NO EXCUSES

NO EXCUSES

How You Can Turn Any Workplace into a Great One

JENNIFER ROBIN
MICHAEL BURCHELL

JB JOSSEY-BASS™
A Wiley Brand

Published by Jossey-Bass
A Wiley Brand
One Montgomery Street, Suite 1200, San Francisco, CA 94104-4594—www.josseybass.com

Jossey-Bass books and products are available through most bookstores. To contact Jossey-Bass directly, call our Customer Care Department within the U.S. at 800-956-7739, outside the U.S. at 317-572-3986, or fax 317-572-4002.

Wiley publishes in a variety of print and electronic formats and by print-on-demand. Some material included with standard print versions of this book may not be included in e-books or in print-on-demand. If this book refers to media such as a CD or DVD that is not included in the version you purchased, you may download this material at **http://booksupport.wiley.com**. For more information about Wiley products, visit **www.wiley.com**.

Library of Congress Cataloging-in-Publication Data

Robin, Jennifer, 1974-
  No excuses : how you can turn any workplace into a great one / Jennifer Robin, Michael Burchell. — First edition.
       pages cm
  Includes index.
    ISBN 978-1-118-35242-7 (hardback), 978-1-118-74694-3 (epdf), 978-1-118-74700-1 (epub)
    1. Corporate culture. 2. Organizational behavior. 3. Employee morale. 4. Work environment. 5. Management. 6. Job satisfaction. I. Burchell, Michael, 1967- II. Title.
  HD58.7.R625 2013
  658.3—dc23

                                       2013022239

Printed in the United States of America
FIRST EDITION
HB Printing   10 9 8 7 6 5 4 3 2 1

Dedicated to the managers and leaders championing great workplaces. We hope you will see this book as an invitation to connect with others so that all of us widen our understanding of what great workplaces are and can be.

CONTENTS

FOREWORD

Somewhat like Nike's infamous "Just Do It" tag line, I'm hopeful that *No Excuses* becomes the calling card of the next generation of managers and leaders seeking to create great workplaces. Jen Robin and Michael Burchell's exploration of their two rules for creating a great workplace—treat every interaction as an opportunity to build trust, and don't resist—provides both guidance and admonishment to spur people forward.

A short, simple phrase, "no excuses" captures the bane of work life for some managers. There's always a reason for not making the effort, for not taking a risk, for doing just enough to get by. The trouble is that all of these excuses for not exerting a little more effort lead to a mediocre workplace rather than one in which people are committed to seeking excellence.

An excuse is somewhat like an apology. Excuses and apologies are comments or stories we share with others that relate to a specific event or action, though an excuse usually comes before any action has been taken and an apology comes after actions have been taken when perhaps things haven't gone so well. A major difference between excuses and apologies is that excuses keep us from doing things while apologies can help us to do things better.

If we learn from our apologies, then we can make improvements. But our excuses stop us in our tracks.

No Excuses is about helping you to do things better and keep moving. After reading this book and implementing the practices presented here, you should actually have fewer apologies to make. That's because Robin and Burchell provide you with a way of moving forward as a manager to create a great workplace environment in your organization that will benefit everyone.

The focus on interactions and opportunities takes everyday encounters and moves them into the future with the question, "What is the opportunity that can come from this moment?" As a manager you can choose to orient your thinking to always consider what could possibly come next. When you do this, you create an opportunity for continuity between your actions and words, your current interactions and the promises that you make—to yourself and others—about the future.

Building trust is all about following through on your promises. So if every interaction is an opportunity to build trust, then every interaction also represents a promise. Which so quickly takes us to Burchell and Robin's second rule: Don't resist. Don't resist the challenge before you. Don't resist the opportunity to make and fulfill your promise, and build a bond of trust.

Don't resist is quite a simple strategy, yet like most concepts that are simple, it is one of the most powerful approaches to effective management that there is. Rather than trying to corral employees, projects, or a whole department to behave according to a complex set of assumptions and expectations about what ought to be, keep it simple. Don't resist the reality of the situation; work with it and build trust.

Why does this work so well as an approach to creating great workplaces? First of all, with a commitment to no excuses, you can focus on making progress and trying things out. Clearly the target for your progress needs to be the creation of a high-trust workgroup or organization. You won't achieve high levels of trust without specifically aiming in that direction. So with high trust as a target, and your commitment to no excuses, you begin the journey.

Most everyone I've ever met in a workplace wants to be part of a great team and a great organization. People will put up with a lot to hold on to their hope that things will get better. When you, as a manager, actually do work hard to make things better, creating trust through every opportunity, the cooperation and commitment you receive in return will more than make up for the extra effort you may be expending to build trust. And when that ball starts rolling forward—no excuses, building trust in every opportunity, and no resistance—you will be able to channel the group's energy toward market opportunities that others let pass them by.

Great workplaces are more successful than others because of the power of trust. Burchell and Robin know this because they have been coaching and consulting with great workplaces for many years, helping managers and leaders to achieve ever greater success. The examples they provide in this book affirm their knowledge by detailing the experiences of managers and leaders in businesses that you know. There are no false stories here, made-up analogies, or fantasy discussions about what might be possible. This is real.

I hope that every reader is as inspired by this book and the examples provided as I have been. And I also hope that everyone commits to taking action based on the excellent guidance provided by Michael and Jen, and all the people they have profiled here. You will become a more effective manager and leader once you start practicing "no excuses" management.

Amy Lyman
Author, *The Trustworthy Leader*
Co-founder, Great Place to Work® Institute

NO
EXCUSES

INTRODUCTION: CREATING A GREAT WORKPLACE

Culture matters. A company's culture determines the limits of its success. Recent surveys conducted by both Pricewater-houseCoopers and IBM assessing the key issues that CEOs face in growing their firms highlight the role of people and culture as crucial to long-term competitive advantage.[1] Organizations today seek the most useful strategies and methods to create a culture of excellence where employees go above and beyond. And decades of research underscore the importance of workplace culture in firm performance.

In 2011, we published *The Great Workplace: How to Build It, How to Keep It, and Why It Matters.* We advanced the idea that creating a great workplace is central to organizing for business success. Based on years of research into the world's best companies, we have found that organizations characterized by a high degree of trust, pride, and camaraderie result in more satisfied and engaged employees. Additionally, these firms also experience an unusually high degree of productivity and financial success. Trust, it turns out, matters.

As a result of that book's publication and reception, we were invited to speak publicly at professional association conferences and more intimately with the managers and leadership teams at a broad range of organizations. As we discussed the model of a great workplace, we found that people were interested and excited. However, when we pressed on to discuss how they could apply the model to their own organization, we were met with some resistance. We found this common pattern of "love the idea, not sure it would work here" curious. We thought, if this sample of managers raised these objections, it stands to reason that many more held similar points of view, and held themselves back from doing the work required to create an environment of trust, pride, and camaraderie in their own work group.

So we tracked the reasons given that our model would not work, and decided to investigate further. Did these reasons constitute real challenges and obstacles? Or were they simply excuses? In our analysis, it's a bit of both. In *No Excuses*, we get into those objections and how to rethink them in light of what we know about the best companies. But first we need to provide some definition to the broad concept of a great workplace. If you've read our first book, you'll just want to skim over this section as a refresher. If you haven't, well, here's a summary of what we have to say about what makes a great workplace in the first place.

THE KNOWLEDGE BASE

Our expertise about great workplaces is based on our affiliation with Great Place to Work® Institute. Our company has been studying great workplaces since its inception in 1991. *FORTUNE* magazine began publishing our list of great workplaces in 1998, and now *FORTUNE*'s 100 Best Companies to Work For® list is released every January in one of the magazine's bestselling issues.

But research into what makes a great workplace began much earlier, in 1980, when co-founder Robert Levering and Milton

Moskowitz were approached by Putnam Publishing to write a book. In their 1984 book, *The 100 Best Companies to Work for in America,* Robert and Milt described the experience of employees at the 100 best workplaces among the hundreds they researched.[2] The *New York Times* bestseller provided informative stories about all 100 companies, and highlighted several aspects they shared, including career opportunities, pay and benefits, and open and honest communication. Themes began to emerge about the characteristics of great workplaces, but what made them that way wasn't as expected.

Turns out that the intuitively obvious prediction, that organizations with the most creative practices and the best bottom lines would be the ones employees raved about, was not universally true. Something was going on that transcended the policies and practices at the best companies to work for. It wasn't *what* their leaders were doing, it was *how* their leaders were doing it. Specifically, the practices companies had, and the money leaders spent on employees, did not always lead to a great workplace; the relationships they built in the process did.

In Levering's 1990 book, *A Great Place to Work: What Makes Some Employers So Good—And Most So Bad,* he discussed great workplaces in terms of relationships.[3] Specifically, he identified the relationships between employees and their leaders, between employees and their jobs, and between employees and each other as the indicators of a great place to work. Relationships at work matter, and in particular, the centrality of these three relationships influenced people's loyalty, commitment, and willingness to contribute to organizational goals and priorities. If leaders implemented practices and created programs and policies that contributed to these three relationships, employees had a great workplace experience. It mattered less what the programs, policies, and practices were, and more that they were done in a way that strengthened relationships.

3

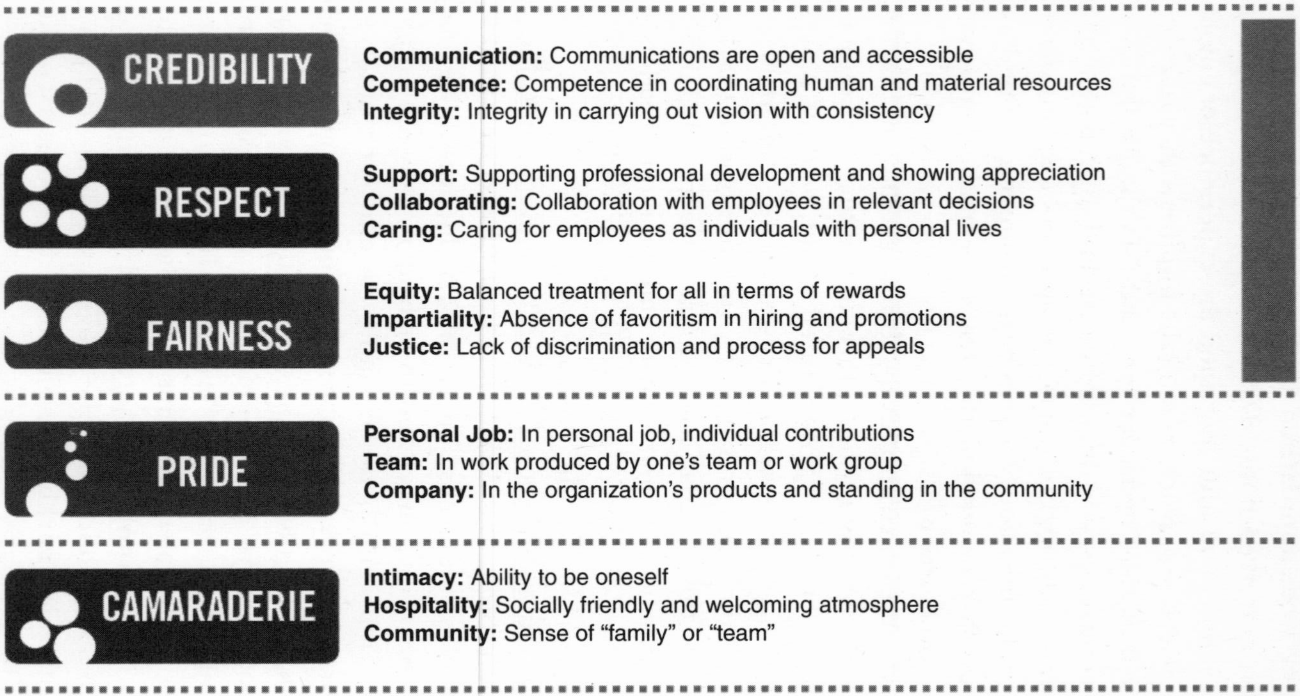

CREDIBILITY

Communication: Communications are open and accessible
Competence: Competence in coordinating human and material resources
Integrity: Integrity in carrying out vision with consistency

RESPECT

Support: Supporting professional development and showing appreciation
Collaborating: Collaboration with employees in relevant decisions
Caring: Caring for employees as individuals with personal lives

FAIRNESS

Equity: Balanced treatment for all in terms of rewards
Impartiality: Absence of favoritism in hiring and promotions
Justice: Lack of discrimination and process for appeals

PRIDE

Personal Job: In personal job, individual contributions
Team: In work produced by one's team or work group
Company: In the organization's products and standing in the community

CAMARADERIE

Intimacy: Ability to be oneself
Hospitality: Socially friendly and welcoming atmosphere
Community: Sense of "family" or "team"

Figure I.1 The Great Place to Work® Model©

The Great Place to Work® Model© (see Figure I.1) was developed as a direct result of this line of research, and later formalized. The model we use today has five dimensions: Credibility, Respect, Fairness (which put together, comprise Trust), Pride, and Camaraderie.

Not only have these five hallmarks stood the test of time, they are also applicable to companies regardless of size or geographic location. The idea of great workplaces and the practical model quickly spread beyond the United States. Now, in over forty countries around the world, the Great Place to Work® Institute has shown that organizations and their employees thrive when these hallmarks are woven into actions on the part of their leaders.

TRUST, PRIDE, AND CAMARADERIE

To set the foundation for our conversation in the chapters to come, it is important that we explicitly define what we mean by a "great place to work." Our definition of a great place to work is one in which you trust the people you work for, have pride in what you do, and enjoy the people you work with.

Trust

When employees in great workplaces talk about the relationship they have with their managers, their comments are quite nuanced, so much so that we can delineate three aspects of the trust relationship that are important to the experience of a great workplace. These are credibility, respect, and fairness.

With regard to the first, employees tend to say that there is effective two-way communication. They also find managers competent and having a clear vision for where the business is going and how to get there. And managers are reliable—they keep their promises and their actions match their words. In short, employees find their managers to be *credible*.

Further, these same employees talk of the support they experience in having the right resources and developmental opportunities to do their job and expand their career. And, when they do a good job, employees are appreciated for a job well done. Beyond this base level of support, managers collaborate with employees on decisions that impact their work—employees are involved in the life of the business. In addition, they feel as if their leaders and managers care about them as people, not just employees; this is often exhibited by expressing care and concern when an employee experiences life challenges, and supports employees in balancing their work life and personal life. In all these ways, employees experience a sense of *respect* by their managers.

Other than credibility and respect, a third component contributes to the trust relationship: *fairness*. This is done by ensuring equity in terms of pay and benefits, and that everyone on the team is seen as a full member. It is also exhibited by being impartial in job assignments and promotions. And, finally, managers develop an inclusive environment, one that is free from discrimination based on personal characteristics.

Pride

Aside from an employee's relationship with their managers, two other relationships are critical. One is the relationship between the individual and his or her work. We call that relationship *pride*. Essentially, people experience a great workplace when they feel as though they make a difference in their organization, that their work is meaningful. They are also proud of both their team's

6

accomplishments and the contributions the organization makes to the community at large.

Camaraderie

The final relationship that employees have is the one they have with their colleagues. This "enjoyment of the people you work with" is expressed through *camaraderie*. Camaraderie exists when employees can be themselves and develop authentic relationships at work. It is bolstered by a warm welcome when employees join the organization or transfer between jobs, and when there is a sense of fun in the work and friendliness among co-workers. Ultimately, camaraderie exists when a sense of community or family is developed.

The dimensions of the Great Place to Work® Model© are exhibited in Figure I.1. This model forms the basis of our understanding of great workplaces.

As intuitively obvious as the model is, it is not a formula. *How* trust manifests or *how* employees experience or express pride differs from one organization to another and from one country to another. The type of policies, practices, and programs that work really well in a toy manufacturing company may not work in a big box retailer. And what camaraderie looks like in Japan is different than in Italy or Mexico or Canada. How enjoyment is experienced by a junior workforce is much different than what more seasoned employees would call a good time. But employees in great workplaces in all types of organizations and in all locations experience trust, pride, and camaraderie. So while the *how* is different, *what* is created—strong relationships—is remarkably consistent all over the world. Because the relationships employees have matter, and you as a manager have a great influence on them, *you* are the critical difference between a very good company and a very great company.

Over time, we've learned a thing or two about creating great workplaces, and while *The Great Workplace* was aimed at sharing what we've learned with you about what they look like, the book you hold in your hands is about doing the hard work to create one of your own. Now that we're clear on what a great workplace is—one where employees trust those they work for, have pride in what they do, and enjoy the people they work with, we can more effectively discuss all the reasons you and other managers might believe they can't do it. Throughout this book, we dig in to the excuses, and help you wipe them out.

In the chapters to follow, we use the term "great workplace" as a shorthand term for the employee experience we discuss above and your efforts to create it. We invite you to read into that shorthand term whatever aspect of a great workplace is meaningful to you in your current role, in your current organization, at the current time. Perhaps you are looking at your workplace environment globally, and you want to take in the entirety of what it means to be a great place to work. Wonderful. Or maybe you are focused intently on the difficulties you find in supporting collaboration with your team, which is an aspect of respect in the model above. That works too! Use the model to frame your thinking about the excuses we will examine in the chapters that follow, and how to address them. We feel strongly that the concept of a great workplace is scalable to your specific work group and your specific concerns.

As we'll remind you throughout this book, our ultimate goal is to start and/or continue a conversation about your workplace. Ideas live in the realm of possibilities, and conversations are the bridge between possibility and action. Visit us at mygreatworkplace.com to join the conversation in progress, or contact us directly if we can help you on your way.

CHAPTER 1

THE ANATOMY OF
AN EXCUSE

You are a manager. Are you good at your job? What if you could be even better? You can create a smart strategy, offer amazing products and services, and be operationally efficient, but unless you can consistently bring out the best in your people, none of that matters. How do you get people to bring their very best to their work and go above and beyond just what's required? You create a great workplace.

There is no more certain avenue of increasing productivity, managing employee engagement, or creating the conditions for collaborative creativity than to create a great place to work. Most successful, experienced managers understand this truism well. The other, equally true statement is that *every* manager and *every* organization can create a great place to work. The trick is in clearing out the obstacles that might keep you from creating such an environment. This book will show you how.

Both of us are affiliated with the Great Place to Work® Institute, a global research, training, and management consultancy. It is best known in the United States for compiling *FORTUNE* magazine's annual list of the 100 Best Companies to Work For®, although the Institute operates and publishes similar lists in over forty countries. As the largest annual study of workplaces, we survey millions of employees in thousands of companies around the world. And we have been engaged in this research for twenty years.

Managers who casually read "best employer" or "great workplace" lists such as *FORTUNE*'s 100 Best Companies to Work For® may deem that, while inspiring or interesting, that lofty of a goal—indeed, that type of work environment— isn't for them. It's as if the workplaces that they read about are fictional, and the list is a way to escape the confines of their own dull organizational life. In actuality the organizations are real, but the workplaces are not perfect. Rather, they are models of a great workplace environment, and while we celebrate their recognition and success, we know that a great workplace is not about list membership. It is about *you*, the manager, and while we hear your excuses, we don't buy them.

Don't get us wrong. We hear you that there may be a lack of commitment and resources for such an effort, or that you are tossed around by the push and pull of organizational demands, that the type of industry or functional area in which you work is different, and so on. It's tough. But, as we will see upon closer scrutiny, these challenges aren't insurmountable if you are dedicated to overcoming them.

Trust our experience and that of consultants like us in Great Place to Work® Institute's forty offices around the globe when we say that "*every* manager can create a great workplace." We have worked with managers responsible for all types of functions such as research and development, manufacturing, customer service, logistics, and sales. These managers come from a diversity of backgrounds in terms of nationality, gender, age, tenure, work history, ethnicity, education, and so on. Some are new, first-time managers and some have been managers for decades. Some are front-line managers and others senior executives. Managers from all across this spectrum have created great workplaces. What this means is that if you have the privilege of managing people, there is no reason you can't create a great workplace.

We also know that any *work group* in any *organization* in any *industry* can be a great workplace. Some of the organizations that make our lists are large technology firms, like Google and Microsoft. Others are industrial firms like Lincoln Industries or Devon Energy. Some are retail operations like Nordstrom or Starbucks and are geographically spread out, and others have a single office like XPLANE. Some are multinational like The Coca-Cola Company, and others are based in a single country, like Futurice in Finland. They cut across industry, size, location, and business model. Think of a company characteristic, and we can find at least one that is a best company somewhere in the world. So, if *any* company can be a great workplace, *every* company can—yours included.

Are there legitimate obstacles that make it a challenge to fully engage your workforce? Sure there are. And we will examine them in this book along with ways of dealing with them. But most of the reasons we hear from managers as to why they cannot create or sustain a great workplace are hurdles, not brick walls.

We know you want to be a successful people manager—you would not still be reading this book if that wasn't the case. If you've run into problems, it's not a lack of desire or interest or hope. We believe that examining perceived obstacles in a clear-headed, no-nonsense fashion is an important step in determining the right course of action.

In order to help you overcome whatever obstacles you may find in your path, we visited ten recognized "best companies to work for" that would offer insight into how they did it. We purposefully selected each of these companies for the type of organization they are. We visited them and met with line managers, HR leaders, and top executives. We researched them thoroughly in advance, examining information we had previously collected from them, as well as reviewing their annual reports and websites. The companies we highlight throughout this book are further described at www.mygreatworkplace.com, but many of them need no introduction:

- Accenture
- Alston & Bird
- Balfour Beatty
- The Coca-Cola Companies
- Devon Energy
- Mayo Clinic
- NetApp
- Teach for America
- Whole Foods Market
- Zappos

We utilized what we learned from these organizations and their managers, along with other research, data, and best practices from the Institute's databases, and our own consulting experience to provide context, insight, and solutions for you as you consider your own workplace.

WHY IT MATTERS

As we noted at the top of the chapter, having a great workplace is good for business. Several studies make clear the business case for increasing trust and creating a great workplace for employees. Some of them even use the best companies lists as their research sample. Faleye and Trahan in their article in the *Journal of Business Ethics*[1] looked at employee productivity, total productivity, profitability, and value. "Consistent with the event study results,"

12

they wrote, "we find that the Best Companies [relative to control panel of S&P 500] outperform comparable firms on all measures. These results are highly robust." The work of Alex Edmans at the Wharton School provides further evidence. In his study, Edmans analyzed the relationship between employee satisfaction and long-run stock performance. He utilized the *FORTUNE* 100 Best Companies to Work For® list over an eight-year period, and even when controlling for other factors (such as risk or industry), found that the 100 Best portfolio earned over double the market returns by the end of 2005. High-trust workplaces consistently outperform lower-trust workplaces.[2]

Indeed, when comparing the best companies to work for with other companies in the same industry, we find that the best companies outperform their peers consistently with regard to financial performance, along with decreased absenteeism, on-the-job injuries, voluntary turnover, shrinkage (in retail), and so on. The graph in Figure 1.1 highlights annualized returns of the publicly traded best companies compared to the S&P 500 since the first

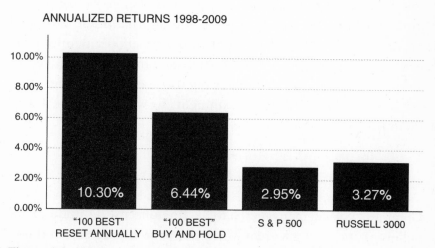

Figure 1.1 100 Best Annualized Returns

FORTUNE list was published. More information about related studies can be found online at www.mygreatworkplace.com.

If you still don't feel like you are the one to create a great workplace in your work group, don't stay stuck. By our measure, you are held back by a combination of two things: an error in framing combined with one or more material challenges in your environment. Both need to be addressed in order to move forward, but it may be helpful to break them apart to understand what you are up against.

NO EXCUSES

This book is called *No Excuses*, because we believe that great workplace leaders take a "no excuses" approach, and we want to help you take that approach.

Within any excuse is a bona fide or material challenge, along with the framing stuff that prevents you from staying out of your own way. While the challenge you may be facing is real, it is not insurmountable. But your attitude and your sense of organizational identity—the way you *frame* your challenge—can fool you into believing it is. Your attitude is the internal frame you need to create a great workplace, and your organization's identity is the best way to frame your external environment. In a way, these two tasks are prerequisites to conquering the material challenges that actually do exist in your environment, so we need to deal with them first.

The Attitude

Great workplace managers have a no-nonsense attitude. They believe that creating a great workplace is both necessary and possible, and they hold themselves responsible for doing so. As Walter

14

Robb, Co-CEO of Whole Foods Market, tells us, "I never like it when people don't take responsibility. It should always be about what can you do, not what can't you do."

This is not to say that doing so is easy or straightforward, and there certainly is no shortage of sleepless nights or heart-wrenching decisions in these managers' lives. But great managers are resolute and confident with periods of being doubtful and indecisive, not the other way around.

As we'll discuss in Chapter 2, managers of great workplaces also have productive beliefs, thoughts, and schemas. They avoid cognitive obstacles to making productive changes in their work environment. Specifically, they believe that success is a product of hard work and effort rather than luck or chance; they have an internal locus of control. Great managers avoid overgeneralizing; they see the nuances in their work environment and they aren't seduced by best practices that just don't fit. Great managers have high aspirations; they don't anchor their own judgments of success too low. And last but not least, great managers are comfortable taking the long view; they don't discount the value of a long-term gain in favor of a short-term win.

The Identity

Equally important is clarity about the organization's identity. Think about any major decision you have ever made and this will ring true. In making that decision, you want your head to be clear; you want the right attitude. But that alone won't suffice. Without also considering your identity—your values, your responsibilities, and your goals—you cannot make a good decision, let alone dedicate yourself to it. The same is true in your organization. Any decision succeeds or fails with regard to how well it reflects and reinforces the best of the organization's identity. When challenges arise, sometimes they do so simply because the manager has lost sight of the organization's identity, not because they are truly insurmountable obstacles.

Remember that great workplace leaders can't set out to build trust independently of the business activities they must carry out on a daily basis. We've seen leaders create task forces and strategic goals and whole departments dedicated to creating a better workplace—to building more trust. But, without giving trust a context, it just doesn't grow. A stand-alone great workplace initiative may get some attention for a while, or serve as a convenient retort when justifying an employee expenditure request, but it doesn't really take hold as part of the fabric of the organization until it is woven into the vision and values, and carried out in the execution of the strategic direction. Keeping these markers of identity top of mind is paramount.

Chapter 3 gives you insight as to what it takes to have a strong sense of organizational identity, and how you might reinforce it over and over again through the way you plan, structure, and execute on your work group's tasks. While an important prerequisite for any great workplace, a strong sense of identity is also necessary to provide ballast as you are attacking the real challenge. When addressing an issue that makes your great workplace tough, you are going to flail and falter, and you will likely get exhausted trying to gain momentum at the outset. A clear sense of your organization's identity creates some stability against which to balance the uncertainty of addressing the big obstacles.

The Challenge

Factor the attitude and the organizational identity out of any excuse and you get a material challenge. In our role as consultants, we too are intimidated and humbled as we help managers get real about facing them. But we are armed with an understanding that the best places to work also face challenges, and they have overcome them. And we believe you can too. Chapters 4 through 9 help you understand how great companies have overcome challenges, and where you might start in doing the same.

In Chapter 4, we'll talk about bad habits and the challenge of inertia that has a bit to do with attitude, but a lot to do with how to put focused effort into shifting behaviors to align better with great workplace ideals. For instance, promoting people based upon tenure long after that is the only way to gain expertise is a bad habit, and an obstacle to building trust. Failing to change habits is a behavioral obstacle from which we'll help you to break free.

In Chapter 5, we'll talk about strategic and operations constraints, and the organizational politics that often travel with them. You know the ones: roles, goals, boundaries, authority, and politics. Wearing multiple hats, addressing competing goals, sharing responsibility with disinterested others—all are hindrances to thinking strategically about your workplace. But none are insurmountable. In fact, the key to your success as a manager is to figure this out—how to be in twelve places at once, while producing superior work, *and* creating a great workplace.

In Chapter 6, we talk about larger organizational and industry forces. As companies in a specific industry go about addressing issues in the marketplace, industry standards take shape that can be at odds with creating a great workplace. It should come as no surprise that every single organization in every single country that has ever made our list of great workplaces has constraints that are hallmarks of their industry. Their leaders just know how to overcome them. You can learn, too.

Unlike the more static challenges that are a consequence of your unique operational environment or your larger industry, disruptive events are more acute, and we deal with those in

Chapter 7. Often, these excuses are prefaced by, "It's just not the right time, because . . . ," followed by lamentations about layoffs, mergers and acquisitions, and leadership changes. We argue that the tough times are actually some of the most important times to build trust, particularly when the alternative is to break it. It is always the right time, and believing otherwise is an excuse.

Remarkably, another great workplace excuse archetype is the people themselves. In Chapter 8, we talk about how to address the real challenges that come from the people who are already on board in the organization, perhaps before a great working environment was a consideration. We've heard that a great workplace will never fly because employees have an entitlement mentality, they live paycheck-to-paycheck, they work part-time or casually, they have low education levels—you name it! Funny that seeing employees as people is one of the hallmarks of a great workplace, but these excuses reflect a tendency to treat them as a group, and therefore an obstacle to a great workplace. As Chip Conley, founder of Joie de Vivre hotels, said in his 2009 *Huffington Post* blog,[3] "Our people will never aspire to more than a job if all they focus on is the fact that they clean toilets in a hotel. But when one sees the broader purpose of what they do, they start to realize their work can fulfill in ways they hadn't imagined. And, the positive result of being in a workplace full of happy fellow employees is noticeable to everyone who comes into contact with an organization." No matter the nature of your workforce, a workplace exists that brings out their best work.

Last but not least, we also address the challenge of leadership in Chapter 9. Probably the most difficult question we are asked is "Can a workplace be great if top leadership is not on board?" The frank answer is that we've never seen a great place to work that didn't have the belief, support, and buy-in of its senior leaders. However, we've also seen great departments, locations, and lines of business that exist within an organization that as a whole isn't really all that great. In Chapter 9, we'll give you everything we've surmised from our experiences with great workplaces and managers who lead them about how to negotiate mixed messages that come from on high.

HOW TO USE THIS BOOK

As you determine how you can best use the material in this book, it may be helpful to review a few of the key ideologies that guide us when we consult with companies hoping to improve the trust, pride, and camaraderie in their workplaces.

Great Workplaces Bring About Better Societies

Though we work hard to demonstrate that there are tangible gains in productivity, time, and money when trust is built, we truly believe that great workplaces bring about better societies. In short, building more trust at work (or in other organizations you lead) is the right thing to do for families, for communities, and for the world at large. When people have work relationships characterized by trust, pride, and camaraderie, their potential for success is greater. And when people feel like they've succeeded, they are more present and giving with their families, more engaged in community activities, and more friendly to the barista who makes their morning latte.

Suspend Your Disbelief

If ever you feel that our perspective on this is a hindrance, we ask that you attempt to suspend your disbelief. Even if you can't get on board with our "right thing to do" notion, can you at least agree that it's not the *wrong* thing to do? And, if that doesn't work for you at some point, skip the section you are reading and move on. We promise we won't spend too much time in the land of milk and honey before returning to the confines of the business world and its challenges, both of which we know you are well accustomed to.

Organizations Are Complex, Living Systems

Organizations are complex, living systems. As such, they will constantly pull toward equilibrium and consistency. Any disruption in the system, including changing your beliefs or behaviors to align with a great workplace, will usually be met with some resistance. Simply put, the only way to sustain the change long enough for it to become the new equilibrium often means changing the adjacent aspects of the system. People, processes, systems, business models, strategies, and organizational culture need to be aligned in order for the change to hold. Thus, if you decide to hire for culture fit, you need to change the interview processes, the interview skills and approach of your managers, the human resource information system (HRIS) that compiles candidate information and ratings, and the performance appraisal model that reinforces those cultural fit characteristics. Of course, all of this assumes that you know what your culture is all about in the first place, and that you are deliberately reinforcing the aspects of your culture that drive productivity.

The result is that moving from a mediocre workplace to a good one, and then from a good workplace to a great one, is never just about changing one thing, or even a small set of things. It is about taking a systems perspective on why the culture is the way it is, how it is reinforced, the business results it produces (or hinders), and the competing priorities associated with it. It's just as much about removing obstacles and changing perspectives as it is altering behavior and creating new ways of working. It's just as much about unlearning as it is learning. We'll guide you through the trees as much as possible, but you should always keep the forest in mind.

What Best Practices Are and Are Not

Best practices are child prodigies. Like a five-year-old piano maestro, best practices are very good at a few things—they inspire, they illustrate, they clarify. But they are not adept at many other things necessary for a company's survival, let alone improvement, when it comes to a great workplace. Consider the following:

- *Best practices aren't recipes.* They should never be adopted wholesale, and they should be evolutions rather than installations. But they can provide us direction and aspiration as we put our own practices into place. Thus, don't roll out an online suggestion system to employees who spend no time in front of computer screens, and refrain from making salaries transparent until you are sure they are fair.
- *Best practices aren't mandates.* They should never be considered "must haves" when it comes to creating a great workplace. But they should help us to consider the nature of our own business model and how it might support and be supported by a practice like the one being articulated. For instance, child care centers or subsidies are seen at many workplaces, but not all of them. The key is that where they

21

are present, they meet a real need of the employees and help to support the trust relationship by providing caring and support.

- *Best practices aren't goals.* They are a means to an end, which is building more trust, pride, and camaraderie in the workplace. When your goal is to launch and maintain a practice like new hire celebrations, you are missing the point. The goal is to make new employees feel welcome and to increase the camaraderie in the work group. That's the goal, not a practice put in place to create it. Frankly, the practice may or may not stand the test of time.

As you read this book, you'll encounter many best practices. We believe that we grow and learn from understanding and conversing about what goes on in great workplaces. We believe that best practices can be incredibly useful to you on your journey . . . when used correctly. On our website, www.mygreatworkplace.com, we'll walk you through how to analyze a best practice in the context of your own work environment, and how to distill the relevant bits for your use. We'll give you an idea of what falling into the trap of treating them like recipes, mandates, or goals looks like, and how to pull yourself out of it. But you need to be vigilant about your use of best practices, and how they are used in other parts of your organization.

Trust Is the Foundation

Last but not least, we believe trust is the foundation. We don't use words like *engagement* to describe a healthy workplace, because engagement is a *result* of high levels of trust. Not the other way around. If you want to influence the results on an engagement survey, you need to do something with your employees and not *to* your employees. If you want to have a reciprocal relationship that shares both the responsibilities and the successes in building a desirable culture and a productive work environment, you build a strong trust relationship, which is a two-way street. Your job as a leader is an important one. You shepherd, steward, facilitate, and champion a great culture. But you don't create it. Rather, you enable everyone to do so.

Using language and ideas that derive from the above key perspectives, you'll find scores of best practices, comments from managers at the best places to work, and our advice. We'll speak like a personal consultant would, showing our understanding of the obstacle by talking about its nature, origin, and impact but then providing thoughts and suggestions for moving past it. We'll illustrate how specific practices can be tailored or taken in spirit and applied to your organization, and we'll provide the most targeted suggestions from the managers we've interviewed. We hope you find yourself in a conversation with us as you read, and that you'll take that conversation to Twitter, LinkedIn, and email if you want us to get even more specific.

As with any good conversation, you may need time to digest the information you receive, match it up with your own experience, and determine which parts of it are the most informative and useful. We invite you to do that. Perhaps you'll skim the book on a bi-coastal flight, but come back to the chapters you find most relevant and engage more deeply with them. We encourage it. Or perhaps you'll be more structured, reading and reflecting deliberately on each chapter. Be our guest.

At the very least, we suggest you read and reflect upon the next two chapters before being more selective. Chapter 2 ensures that your attitude is a productive one, and it helps to clear out the cobwebs of what the late motivational speaker Zig Ziglar is famous for calling "Stinkin' Thinkin'." Chapter 3 asks that you take a hard look at your vision, values, and strategic imperatives. Make sure they provide the elusive mix of stability and inspiration that any workplace culture change needs.

Excuses are really just difficulties dressed up in cognitive challenges and a lack of clarity about your organization's identity. Adjust your attitude, understand and align with the organization's identity, and those difficulties become challenges that seem a bit more manageable. They won't be easy by any stretch, but we know you can overcome them. Begin with this: On the other side of the challenges is a great workplace, and there is no longer an excuse to stay paralyzed in anything but.

CHAPTER 2

I THINK [LIKE A GREAT WORKPLACE LEADER], THEREFORE I AM [A GREAT WORKPLACE LEADER]

Your brain is an amazing thing. It makes up only 3 percent of your body weight, yet uses 20 percent of the energy your body expends in its day-to-day functioning. Most of that energy your brain uses is spent generating 70,000 thoughts per day.[1] The first step to creating a great workplace is to ensure that the portion of those thoughts dedicated to how you think about the work ahead of you is constructive. Just as Descartes points out in his pontification, "I think, therefore I am," your attitude toward great workplaces is your ticket toward one.

We've known for a long time that the attitude of leaders in an organization makes the biggest difference between plateauing at "pretty good" and reaching "great" when it comes to their workplace environment. That makes sense when you think about the fact that relationships are what really matter. It's no longer *what* you do in a good environment; it's *how* you do it in a great one. A leader's attitude toward people will dictate that *how*, and ultimately the quality of the relationships in the workplace.

It's not the fact that you offer a leave of absence for employees who wish to dedicate their time and energy to one of their passions outside of work. That's the *what*, or the policy itself. Rather, like Accenture's "Future Leave," you allow employees to bank salary each week that will support them financially during the leave. That extra step on the part of Accenture's leaders, the piece that costs a little in administrative and coordination costs, is the how that makes all the difference for employees. As a result, employees at Accenture can take a leave of absence knowing that there is a financial cushion to support them during that time. If you care about your employees, you will not only offer a great benefit like Future Leave, but you will go out of your way to make sure they can use it. The difference it makes to employees may not be quantifiable, but leaders in great companies believe that it matters; otherwise they'd forgo the expense and efforts in coordination. Leaders in great workplaces have the kind of attitude that will help them reach (and then maintain) greatness in their workplace, and that attitude includes a basic trust in relationships that is not always evidenced in a cost/benefit analysis.

Sometimes in our meetings with great leaders, we do a little role playing. We ask them to pretend we are colleagues in their industry, and we want to move our firm from good to great. We then ask for specific guidance and behavioral guidelines to help us do so. Surprisingly, these leaders have a hard time articulating the specific steps, because it's like a fish recognizing water. Their mindset is primary, and all behavior flows from that. After some conversation, they're able to lay out some specific steps, but their first response is typically one that refers to having the correct mindset.

Take Richard Hays, Managing Partner of Alston & Bird. He says, "I think you communicate to your leadership team that these are the priorities of the firm, this is what we believe in, and this is why we believe it. You have to connect it to the success of the business enterprise because if it's viewed separately, it will lose impact. It can't be viewed as a nice add-on."

Or take Mary Edwards, Client Account Executive at Accenture, who says, "I guess I don't understand why someone might say that there's no time for trust, pride, and camaraderie. I think trust is about the way in which you interact with people and whether they can count on you. Accenture is an environment where you make commitments and you keep your commitments. It's not about time. It's just in our culture—you keep your commitments. I remind people all the time that they don't want to be remembered for things they commit to but don't deliver on."

While their comments are helpful, they're not exactly specific. That's because these leaders, who are nothing if not sharp and articulate, are almost baffled by the question "How do I get started?" Our conclusion is that they are understandably taken aback because the way you get started isn't by changing anything in your work environment at all; rather, it's by changing your mind.

To sum up the perspective that it takes to be a great workplace: "Treat every interaction as an opportunity to either build trust or break it down, and always choose the path that builds trust." We typically anticipate a couple of arguments with that statement, and so we offer our counterpoints below.

First, can all interactions really send messages about culture? All interactions serve as artifacts of culture. So, yes.

Ed Schein, the premier researcher in the area of organizational culture, focuses heavily on the influence of artifacts when it comes to communicating shared values and norms and making meaning of organizational events.[2] Virtually anything can serve as an artifact, from how people are arranged in the physical work environment to the ways in which people communicate good news. At Balfour Beatty Construction, based in Dallas, a long-cherished company tradition was the "ringing of the [cow] bell"—a signal to employees that they'd just been awarded a new construction contract. People from all departments and divisions would head to the reception area to hear about the new job. With the advent of the Internet, that practice has changed a bit, with an email sent to employees announcing each new contract. Regardless of its form, this artifact signals an expansive view of "team," where a contract means that everyone wins, not just those who sold it. It may not have great meaning from the outside looking in, but inside the walls of Balfour Beatty Construction, it is a signal that they work hard and play hard, and that celebrating is a big part of their company culture.

By way of further illustration, in *Fast Company*'s July/August 2012 issue, editors asked people "Is your manager a creativity killer?" One response went something like this: "My boss has a mug with a quote from Henry Matisse on it: 'Creativity takes courage.' I love it when he brings it to meetings and spends the whole time shouting and browbeating us. He's not being ironic; he's being an ass."[3] The mismatch between artifacts confuses the message, which breaks trust in and of itself. But, if he follows the rule above and treats *every* interaction as an opportunity to build trust, he aligns with the coffee cup.

The second anticipated argument: Aren't there trust-neutral interactions? We can't know for sure, but it doesn't matter. Don't treat them that way and you'll build a great workplace. That brings us back to mindset. As you read this book, you may think of policies to roll out that help to build trust. We encourage it. You may also set an intention to behave differently, with all of the trappings of a specific, measurable, and timely goal creation and a coach or other accountability partner to hold you to it. Do that too. But you can put hundreds of practices into place, and you can commit to thousands of behavior changes, but you won't be able to account for every interaction within every turn of events. Adopt the right mindset instead, which is to always choose the path that builds trust.

We are reminded of a practice at Vanderbilt University, a 2009 *FORTUNE*'s 100 Best Companies to Work For list-maker. Their leadership development program is called "Elevate," and one manager told us that when it was necessary in her department, they reminded each other to "elevate" their behavior by gently raising their hands up and down. What struck us about this practice, and why we share it now, is that it reminds people of a way of thinking, rather than a specific behavior. Her team didn't enumerate all the ways in which day-to-day behavior was either in or out of alignment with Elevate's leadership lessons; rather, they use the non-verbal reminder to call people back to a *way of thinking* about how people are expected to relate to one another.

As easy as changing your approach to creating a great workplace may sound, you need to be aware of some very real challenges to doing so. Pardon us while we get technical for a second, but time and time again in our consulting work, we see examples of self-defeating beliefs, dysfunctional thinking, and rigid schemas that were first identified by psychologists such as Albert Ellis, Aaron Beck, and David Burns. Essentially, these experts tell us that our repeated ways of thinking about our world can be skewed, which is dangerous when those patterns of thinking drive much of our reactions to our world (broadly) and our workplaces. We have a lot to learn from these theorists about the cognitive patterns that keep us stuck, and ultimately about changing the way we think. Ultimately, these psychologists put forth a model of psychological health that rests upon an individual's automatic and constructive beliefs and thoughts. By extension, we can look at the health of the workplace as a function of the beliefs of its leader. Fix the thinking, and you are on your way to fixing the workplace.

In this chapter, we inventory four of the most relevant dysfunctional (or counter-functional, in some cases) beliefs and schemas, along with examples of how they might show up in your own great workplace efforts. For short, we call these dysfunctional beliefs and schemas "cognitive obstacles." We also give you some guidance as to how to change the cognitive obstacles as they apply to your organization, and how to establish the productive thought patterns that are more aligned with those we see in great workplace leaders.

"GREAT WORKPLACES ARE BORN THAT WAY"

Probably the most fundamental cognitive obstacle that keeps leaders stuck is the idea that great workplaces are somehow born that way, that their leaders create and maintain a great workplace more easily due to luck or circumstance rather than hard work or effort. When we hear it, it typically comes in the form of a lamentation about the unlucky and opposite circumstance in the leader's organization. Take the following:

- "We aren't located in a great city."
- "Our industry is really suffering."
- "Our workforce is unionized."
- "Our products really don't attract good people."
- "We're too small."

Later in the book, we'll discuss how to handle each of these admittedly difficult challenges to creating a great workplace. But the first step is to realize the cognitive obstacle at play here: external locus of control.

Julian Rotter is an American psychologist who is well known for his work developing the notion of "locus of control."[4] In his conceptualization, individuals with an external locus of control believe that outcomes are a result of chance, fate, or luck, under the control of powerful others, or unpredictable due to the complexity of forces contributing to those outcomes. Psychologist Bernard Weiner[5] added that extraordinary task difficulty might also lead individuals to adopt an external locus of control. Alternatively, individuals with an internal locus of control believe that outcomes are a result of their behavior or relatively permanent characteristics.

Study after study has shown that an internal locus of control is related to greater performance, goal achievement, and job satisfaction.[6] This makes intuitive sense in that if people believe that favorable outcomes are a result of their own effort, they're more likely to try to attain them. Likewise, if a leader believes that his or her hard work leads to a great workplace, he or she is more likely to take action to create one.

Accordingly, the cognitive obstacle at play here is to believe that a great workplace is due to luck or chance. The belief great leaders adopt instead is that they can influence the workplace and create a great one. Note that these cognitions are automatic. In other words, you will need to make the constructive internal locus of control just as strong, if not a stronger habit than the external locus of control. Ceree Eberly, Chief People Officer at The Coca Cola Company, says it this way: "As a business now 127 years strong, we continually are going through change and transformation. Our role as leaders is to help people think about the possibilities—new ways of operating, new ways of working together that will help our consumers and customers, and new ways to become more effective. That has meant asking people to think 'why not?' and asking them to envision their world differently. It's not always easy for people to have to consider 'why change' when things have worked in the past."

You need two things to keep the "luck" obstacle at bay. First, you need to be self-aware and honest, recognizing when the external locus is rearing its head. Share your desire to shift your locus of control with a mentor or significant other. They can often help you identify this cognitive obstacle and set you on a path to a more internal locus. Beyond awareness, you need to find a way to exist comfortably between two contradictory beliefs: 1) you have the power to change your environment and 2) there are limits to how much and how quickly you can change. Accurate information will help you with the first, and realistic goals will help with the second. To illustrate with a silly example, your humble authors can become better basketball players, as long as we have accurate information about what it takes to do so. But, we also need to realize that we will never become NBA players, due to very real limitations of age, gender, and height. Your workplace goals are also within your reach, as long as you know what it takes to achieve them and what they will look like when you do.

Accurate Information

In a word, great workplaces are *work*. Their leaders are always aiming to maintain, if not improve, the workplace environment despite challenges that seem insurmountable. Chuck Tanner, a reservoir manager at Devon Energy, drove this point home when he spoke about the challenge of growth and how he approaches it by developing his people. "This year, we'll be bringing online 380 new wells. Time management and getting things approved in a timely manner is a challenge. Periodically, I appoint someone to coordinate a process, whether that be budget, reserves or our portfolio modeling. Although it's more work for these typically younger engineers, it provides a broader perspective on our business and develops leadership skills. I think it's a good way to leverage my time and helps develop other people's skills." It's work to deal with growth, but this manager finds a way to deal with it while developing people.

Similarly, Chris Nielsen, CFO and COO of Zappos, talks about maintaining the special culture of Zappos after the company was acquired by Amazon. "In one of the first conversations I had here, we talked about a set of principles that we would use to define our relationship with Amazon. We wrote those down and we still refer to them. The gist of it is that we recognize that Zappos is a unique place, we want to retain that uniqueness and we'll work hard to do that." Being acquired is a material threat to the strongest of organizational cultures, but Zappos did not shy away from the challenge of maintaining it.

Acknowledging that creating a great work environment is, in fact, work, will help to normalize your experience and inoculate against defaulting back to the sense that your horrible workplace is due to bad luck when things get difficult. It is easy to abandon your hard-earned internal locus of control when the chips are down, so the more information you have about what it takes, the better. We also encourage you to ask other managers about their experiences, but take care to focus as much (if not more) on the actions to overcome the challenges rather than the challenges themselves. Ask, "What is going well?," "What is your big workplace success this week?," and "How did your efforts help to create it?"

Realistic Goals and Expectations

Once you truly believe you can influence your workplace environment, you also need to take care not to overdo it. While you can control much more than you likely think you can, you will need to set realistic goals and expectations moving forward. Failing to achieve goals that are too expansive, or failing to define goals in a way that allows you to observe success, reinforces an external locus of control. Several years ago, we worked with a leader who wanted desperately to have informative and lively town hall meetings . . . and he wanted them immediately. It only took one failed attempt—trying to solicit questions in real time from the audience and getting awkward silence in response—for him to realize he had overstepped his capabilities. When that happens, especially if your internal locus is shaky, it's easy to revert back to the notion that leaders with successful town hall meetings are just lucky.

Start small and you insulate yourself from that unfortunate (yet very human) response. A better first step would be to solicit anonymous questions, or at the very least, ask that they be written on index cards and passed to a moderator. Remember, though, that some obstacles are not cognitive. They are material. In this example, the cognitive obstacle (belief that he could lead an effective town hall meeting) had already been removed. The failure to set realistic goals was the larger problem, and we'll talk about these more material challenges in the second part of this book. Suffice it to say for now, our fearless town hall leader did not consider the material obstacle of habit (addressed in Chapter 4) or the nature of employees themselves (discussed in Chapter 8).

In sum, an internal locus of control means adopting the notion that for some situations you can't do *everything*, but that doesn't mean you shouldn't do *anything*.

"GREAT WORKPLACES ALWAYS HAVE [INSERT PRACTICE HERE]"

Related to external locus of control is the notion that great workplaces are created by following a fairly standard recipe. Therefore, if leaders don't have the requisite ingredients, a great workplace is unattainable. When we speak to leaders, they are often surprised to learn that only about one-third of the companies that appear on *FORTUNE's* 100 Best Companies to Work For® annual list have on-site childcare. And a mere 14 percent have fully paid health benefits. Far from formulaic, great workplaces become great due to their own unique approach. Assuming that there is "one best way" can slip you into an external locus of control pretty quickly, particularly if your organization cannot afford the time or physical space to initiate a specific program.

More importantly, though, this cognitive obstacle can lead to the creation of a gallery of loosely related best practices rather than an integrative and holistic employee experience. We worked with a company that, taking a cue from the best workplaces, put into place a state-of-the-art online training platform, complete with hundreds of modules, a career planning curriculum builder, and a "transcript" of sorts that could be used to make promotion and internal transfer decisions. The system was beautiful . . . and woefully underutilized. Employees at this organization were never in front of their computers long enough to focus on an online training module, and even if they were able to get a good start, they were likely interrupted before they could finish. Moreover, the type of employees attracted to this organization was much more relational and hands-on than an online education system would support.

The technical name for this obstacle is *overgeneralization*, and it may take many forms. At its core, overgeneralization stems from the learning process of generalization—we think about new experiences in terms of our old experiences. To successfully learn, individuals continue to discover differences between the new experience and the old one, and their understanding becomes more and more nuanced. Overgeneralization, however, occurs when you stop observing the nuances and you assume that all new experiences (i.e., your great workplace) are fundamentally the same as old ones (i.e., list-making great workplaces). In the case of the company's online training, overgeneralizing resulted in a lost opportunity to create a system that would be more appealing to the organization's employees and more aligned with its culture.

Our experience as consultants has taught us never to stop looking for nuances in the ways in which leaders imagine and create their great workplaces. Year after year, list after list, we watch with wide-eyed wonder to see what innovative practices and programs inspire trust, pride, and camaraderie in employees. The only constant is that the innovations are uniquely matched to the nuances of the organization; they are not a replica of another organization's practice.

We were struck by this appreciation when talking with Jill Ragsdale, Chief HR Officer at Mayo Clinic. She told us, "One of my first few weeks, I stepped back and sketched for myself a document that tracked the connection between Human Resource programs and the Mayo Clinic culture. As I looked at the HR processes, it became clear to me that by changing any one of them, we could unintentionally harm what has become the Mayo culture or we could solidify it. If you look at our pay systems, we're not a merit-based pay system for allied health staff. Our performance reviews ask if you meet performance expectations or not, and we don't link that into a pay program. Within a job category, the increases are equally distributed." This egalitarian approach to pay would not fly at many companies, but the leaders at Mayo Clinic don't overgeneralize what they know about practices in other hospitals. Instead, Jill and others see their organization as nuanced and unique, and they implement practices to reinforce the team-based, collaborative environment that makes Mayo Clinic a success.

Paradoxically, overgeneralization can hamper your efforts in other ways as well. It is easy to assume that the best workplaces get that way by implementing complex, novel employee relations practices, particularly when many of the publishers of great workplace lists showcase these practices. Great Place to Work® Institute's lists take into account the totality of practices in the workplace, from the novel to the mundane. However, when it comes to publishing the list, town hall meetings and mentoring programs (veritable staples in each year's lists of recognized companies) often don't get much publicity. While one more news bite about the potential trust-building features of a "New Hire Breakfast" will not sell many magazines, that doesn't mean those simple practices should be overlooked when creating your great workplace. Simple is at the heart of many great workplace attitudes when it comes to building trust; straightforward relationships between the identity of the organization and the practice put into place to build trust within its walls are the antidote to overgeneralization. So don't have a meeting where everyone tries to think of a clever HR activity that no company has ever done before. Think instead of what works for you, even if it's simple.

"WE'RE NOT AS GOOD AS SOME, BUT WE'RE BETTER THAN OTHERS"

One of the many truisms that Jim Collins has given us is "Good is the enemy of great."[7] Of course, this is because good is a signal that we can stop, rest, and work on something that is in more urgent need of our attention. In our work, we see this malaise all too often. Not surprisingly, a cognitive obstacle is at the root of this as well. All of us assess our environments using an anchor, or standard. "Today is colder than yesterday" or "I am here early" are everyday examples of this. But as a cognitive obstacle, *anchoring* is the term given when that standard is faulty in some way. Collins would say, and we agree, that "good" is a faulty anchor, because it leaves potential on the table. And therein we have our next cognitive obstacle: Is your anchor in the right place?

The best way to understand this obstacle is to consider the research of Dan Ariely. In one of his studies, described in the *Huffington Post*, Ariely and his colleague asked MBA students to write down the last two digits of their social security number (which ended up serving as the "anchor") in this study. Then, the students bid on several items in a silent auction–type exercise. The main question Ariely wanted to answer was if the arbitrary anchor of the individual social security numbers would influence the MBA students' bidding behavior. As he puts it: "Remarkably, they did: the students with the highest-ending social security digits (from 80 to 99) bid highest, while those with the lowest-ending numbers (1 to 20) bid lowest. In the end, we could see that students with social security numbers ending in the upper 20 percent placed bids that were 216 to 346 percent higher than those of the students with social security numbers ending in the lowest 20 percent."[8]

Where you anchor your view of success matters, and leaders in great workplaces drop their anchors in lofty places. While they take a measured view of just how quickly they'll get there, leaders with whom we spoke weren't planning to take a break anytime soon. Ceree Eberly, Chief People Officer at The Coca Cola Company, told us just that when she said, "One of our most important leaders, Robert Woodruff, said, 'The future belongs to the discontented.' At Coca-Cola, we're our own worst critics. We're never satisfied with what we do because we always want to do better. The quote is a reminder that we can never become arrogant. That's one of the things about being a 127-year-old company—if you rest easily on your laurels you can lose sight of your market, your consumers and your customers. They're changing faster than we are. We have to always reinvent what we do and how we do it to remain relevant." Eberly describes an anchor that is not only lofty; it is a moving target! Consequently, managers hearing this message will keep aspiring to make workplaces better long after they reach today's goal.

One of the questions we often get from managers is, "What separates #1 from #100 on *FORTUNE*'s 100 Best Companies to Work For® annual list?" The answer is, frankly, not much. What they are really asking is if they can lower the bar a bit to shoot for list membership rather than list domination. Likewise, the real answer is, frankly, no. The best get there because they are always challenging themselves to be even better. All of the companies on the list, and many companies we evaluate for the list, have leaders with few cognitive obstacles, a keen understanding of their organization's identity (as we'll discuss in the next chapter), and consistent efforts to address the challenges of their particular industry, location, size, etc. Their practices may be different, and more or less aligned with their identity, but in our experience they don't anchor themselves against the external environment more than they attempt to best themselves.

This is not to say learning from others isn't a good idea. On the contrary, we believe in the power of best practices. But we also know that attempting to hit an external target of some sort is a sure-fire way for an organization to lose its way, both as a great workplace and as a marketplace competitor. At the Great Place to Work® Institute annual conference in 2009, John Pazzani, Chief Culture Officer at Timberland, told a small audience that "for the first time since [*FORTUNE*'s annual list of Best Companies to Work For®] has been published, we've dropped off the list. What I believe has happened is that we lost sight of who we were. As an organization, we didn't focus on ourselves; we focused more externally than we should have."

Your way through this obstacle is to set an aspirational anchor. Don't stop at "good" or even "very good." What would it take to get your workplace to great? And, folding in the lessons about the other two obstacles, you must also realize that you will get there through hard work (i.e., adopting an internal locus of control) and by honoring the uniqueness of your workplace (i.e., avoiding overgeneralization).

"RESOLVED: WE WILL BE A GREAT WORKPLACE BY TOMORROW"

Immediate gratification. Though we talk about it as the downfall of the younger generation, the source of divisiveness in politics, and the root of unwise business practices from shady deals to layoffs, let's face it: We want things now. And why shouldn't we? Technologies developed in the past three decades have put information literally at our fingertips. While it has probably become a part of the background when you run a Google search, the top of every search page still reports a statistic like: "About 1,700,000 results (0.16 seconds)." Immediate gratification is insidious, and part of the underlying set of expectations we have about any result we seek, including a great workplace.

If you haven't already guessed by now, the bedrock of this phenomenon is also a well-researched cognitive obstacle. *Hyperbolic discounting*,[9] studied by economists and psychologists alike, refers to the human tendency to prefer a short-term payoff to a long-term one, even if the long-term payoff is better. In the case of a great workplace, the long-term payoff is a great workplace, characterized by trusting relationships that are often beyond the realm of a cost/benefit analysis. So, in a double whammy of sorts, you must shift the cognitive obstacle to a belief that the investment of time and effort in a long-term, unquantifiable outcome is better than a quick win financially.

Take the example of NetApp, a U.S.-based multinational computer storage and data management company. NetApp actually saw results *decrease* after the first year of focusing on becoming a great workplace. They kept going, and have reached the #1 spot in the U.S. on *FORTUNE*'s 100 Best Companies to Work For® list, not to mention membership on the list of the World's Best Multinational Workplaces. If NetApp would have abandoned ship after failing to achieve any short-term progress, they would not have been the workplace success they are now known to be all over the world.

More and more we are seeing publically traded companies take a longer view despite pressures from the market analysts to consistently turn a short-term profit. Unilever, a multinational consumer goods company that appears on several great workplace lists worldwide, has an impressive sustainability program that will only succeed if the focus is on the long-term outcomes. In an interview with HBR IdeaCast, CEO Paul Polman said, "We've created an environment for our business to be a little bit more longer-time focused. We abolished quarterly profits."[10] While Polman understands that a long-term effort is still effort, he also notes the positive impact this shift in perspective has had on the operations of his organization. "It . . . allowed us in the company to have our business people do the right things. We don't manipulate, now, the advertising spent by quarter or other things. But I dread, to be honest, a six-month period that our results are not so good, because the cynics will come out and the critics will come out. That is for sure. But we need to be strong enough to work our way through that when that happens."

Of all the cognitive obstacles, this one may be the most difficult to hold in check, simply because the pressures to return immediate results are not only human nature, but reinforced by our financial markets and in turn, our leaders. Luckily, there is nothing wrong with quick wins when it comes to creating a great workplace, as long as they don't damage the possibility to continue to build trust over the long term. We often encourage leaders to look for those areas where they can gain some immediate ground in building better relationships with employees, simply because it provides momentum and energy to persist during the long journey ahead. Perhaps the best way to keep hyperbolic discounting in check is to balance it, always, with longer-term thinking.

REFLECTION

Aside from the specific ways we've discussed to overcome the four cognitive obstacles and create new mental habits, there is one more recommendation that we'd be remiss if we didn't discuss in the context of cognitive readiness for building a great workplace. It is the deceptively simple act of reflection. Of course, reflection helps you to be more aware of cognitive obstacles as they present themselves, but both academics and the managers we interviewed talked about an additional benefit to doing so. Specifically, they call attention to the value of taking a step back to consider the impact of decisions and, by extension, the messages that they send to employees about culture.

In a 2002 article by Heike Bruch and Sumantra Ghoshal called "Beware the Busy Manager," they note that only 10 percent of managers they study are purposeful, or capable of both focus and energy.[11] (In the next chapter, we'll discuss what these two characteristics look like at a work group or organizational level.) They included a telling quote from manager who fell into the purposeful category: "In the busiest times, I slow down and take time off to reflect on what I actually want to achieve and sort what's important from irrelevant noise," he says. "Then I focus on doing what is most important." The paradox is striking—in the busiest times, one may need to slow down in order to ensure a focus on what's most important.

We'd recommend using reflection on your present and past to ensure the right attitude going forward, but take care to reflect upon your role in the organization as well. That is, be clear about your perspective on leadership, and how your position in the organization brings you a sense of meaning. Then you can bring that same sense of meaning to others in the form of a great workplace. We asked Dr. John Noseworthy, CEO of Mayo Clinic, what advice he may give a young physician about behaviors to adopt or things to start learning now that may be helpful down the road should that physician step into the role of CEO. Dr. Noseworthy recounted his words to a group of young physicians: "The overriding message I gave to them is that the most important thing for a bright young person to do is to be reflective. I said to them, 'Your whole career is ahead of you. Reflect carefully; get to know yourself.'"

How you engage in reflection is up to you, but we have found that your methods shouldn't feel like work. Rather, they should capitalize on your natural inclinations. If you enjoy writing, journal. If you like the outdoors, take a hike. If you are better reflecting out loud, enlist a trusted partner to listen and mirror your thoughts back to you. The means you choose matters less than the ends it produces.

The hold that the four obstacles have on your progress toward a great workplace will likely abate simply by your awareness of them. Make it a practice to reflect upon the attitudes you'd like to bring to your work as a manager in a great workplace and the meaning it brings to you personally, and you've guaranteed that the cognitive obstacles many struggle with will no longer stand in your way.

In sum, step one in creating a great workplace is to clear the cognitive obstacles. Reflect. Realize that it is your effort and hard work that will create a great workplace, not luck or chance. Treat your workplace as a unique environment that needs integrated and coherent practices in order to build trust, not as a blank canvas on which you can plug and play practices that you find intriguing. Set lofty goals, and don't settle for "very good." And, last but not least, adopt a long-term focus that allows you to invest in trusting relationships rather than gamble on short-term financials.

Are there other cognitive obstacles? Sure. But these are the four we hear most often, and those that can be the most ominous when we talk with managers long enough to size up their chances of creating a great workplace. Changing the way you think is the first step, and then you can tackle the business of adopting an organizational identity and dealing with the challenges that are real.

In the next chapter, we'll talk about the second foundational aspect of your great workplace, understanding and adopting a sense of organizational identity. Without it, you don't have the stability to take on the big challenges to a healthy workplace culture.

CHAPTER 3

WE ARE WHAT WE REPEATEDLY DO

NetApp is in the highly competitive technology industry. They have over 13,000 employees in over 150 offices around the world, and NetApp was named one of the best multinational workplaces in the world in 2012. One of the distinguishing characteristics of NetApp, reinforced throughout our interviews with managers, was the consistency with which they understand who and what their company is and is not. Like Aristotle's maxim about being what we repeatedly do, it seemed that regardless of their role or location, managers spoke in strikingly similar terms about the vision of the organization, the workplace culture, and their business model.

NetApp's TOAST (or Training On All Special Things that all new hires attend) made an appearance several times in our conversations, and it is one mechanism NetApp uses to create a shared sense of identity. TOAST is a full-day new hire orientation that is led by the CEO and his immediate executive team. Employees spend a full day with the CEO and his team learning about the culture, values, history, and business strategy. They have lunch with Tom, and an executive is at each table, and there is a Q&A session at the end of the day that gives employees a chance to ask their most challenging questions. One manager shared that "to me, TOAST was kind of like when you get initiated into a fraternity or sorority. I felt so empowered the day after because I couldn't believe that all these people took time out of their busy schedules and talked to us about the company and how they see it." Observed another, "Two months ago, we flew an entire team here for TOAST. It's not something that just happens at headquarters. Through the hyper-growth, it's important to establish [a common sense of purpose] from day one. I think it starts there and it's really important." Common culture practices form a basis for a shared organizational identity.

NetApp is not dissimilar to the other best companies we interviewed. Each of the best companies has a very strong sense of organizational identity—who they are, what defines them, how they operate, and what their culture is. There is shared understanding and language, and a similar approach to how they look at the world around them.

Having a strong sense of organizational identity, then, empowers managers and breaks down potential barriers to effectively creating a great workplace. The opposite is also true. A weak sense of an organization's identity makes it challenging to take effective action. When this happens, managers seek to explain their inability to be as successful as they might otherwise be. In other words, they use excuses.

In this chapter, we will first look at the component aspects of an organization's identity. These include the things that give meaning and direction to a company such as its mission, vision, and values. It also includes the aspects that provide structure, such as the business strategy and management system. The most subtle part of an organization's identity is its workplace culture as it shapes how work actually gets done. Next, we will turn to the typical reasons why an organizational identity isn't used more effectively by managers. And finally, we will turn to the requirements for understanding and mobilizing your organizational identity as you create a great workplace.

BASIC ELEMENTS OF AN ORGANIZATIONAL IDENTITY

There is an old Zen saying, "After enlightenment, the laundry," which beautifully captures the idea that one can never let go of the minutiae that helped enable the enlightened state in the first place. All of us have "life management" tasks such as purchasing groceries, paying bills, and doing laundry that are necessary to organize our life and that help facilitate other higher-order things such as engaging in meaningful work or connecting with loved ones. The same is true in business. We need to get the basics right and do the organizational laundry.

Our view of "organizational laundry" is having a clearly articulated mission and vision, values that guide the organization, an effective strategy, a productive management system, and a workplace culture that supports all of this. We too often find, however, organizations operating without reference to the basics. Quickly, the vision becomes a slogan, the business plan becomes a doorstop, and the values are a plaque on the wall. Conversely, in great workplaces, we find that behind their financial success lies a strong sense of identity that helped create such excellence in the first place.

Through our experience, it has become clear that only in addressing these areas of "organizational laundry" can you really leverage the power and opportunity that comes from creating and sustaining a great workplace. But as mundane as the laundry sounds, it can be energizing. As long as your effort helps to reinforce the sense of organizational identity, it contributes to a great workplace and buffers against the inertia of excuses. At W. L. Gore

& Associates, they talk about their "one objective," which is "to make money and have fun." As a business, they understand that they need to make money or they won't have a business for long. Yet, they also appreciate that having fun together as they accomplish their goals builds an enduring business for the long term. Both need to be in balance, and at Gore, they work diligently in meeting their one objective. And as a result, Gore is a very solid business.

No matter what form they take, an adage such as that at W. L. Gore & Associates or a more formal statement, best companies have a clear mission, vision, and values first and foremost. Second, they have a well-crafted strategy or plan for achieving their vision and goals. Third, they have created the right management structure to align their internal resources in service of that vision. And fourth, they have developed a strong, sustainable, high-trust workplace culture that enables its employees to deliver on that vision.

These four points are summed up well by Rajeev Peshawaria in *Brains, Bones, and Nerves: The Only Three Things an Enterprise Leader Should Focus On*, an online publication by 800-CEO-READ.[1] In it, he explains that there are a vital few things an enterprise leader should focus on. He offers, "The key is to control and shape the three most important levers of sustainable business growth—the brains, the bones, and the nerves. The brains of a business are its vision and strategy, and here the enterprise leader must shape and set direction. The bones are the organizational architecture, and here the enterprise leader must design the organization in order to execute the strategy. And the nerves refer to the culture and climate of the organization, and here the enterprise leader must foster a culture of long-lasting excellence."

At The Coca-Cola Company, they have been able to capture the "brains, bones, and nerves" onto a single-page document that all managers and all employees have access to, understand, and use in their work. The Coca-Cola Company sees its mission as refreshing the world, inspiring moments of optimism and happiness, creating value, and making a difference. The Coca-Cola system comprises both the company that owns the brands and produces the beverage bases as well as the network of more than 250 bottling partners around the world. The culture is focused on creating a great place to work across the entire system.

As one of the managers we spoke with at Coca-Cola explained, "There's a visionary document that looks ten years ahead with six P's including profit, people, portfolio, partners, planet and productivity. Everybody in the organization knows they play a very important role and their company's performance is continually tracked in each of the P's. This is a phenomenal strategy that took us some time to put in place, and now the culture is following this." It took The Coca Cola Company some time to align to their plan, but now they are really beginning to see the payoff for doing this organizational laundry—and creating a great workplace in the process.

Mission, Vision, and Values

Best companies understand why they exist, what they are trying to achieve, and how they will go about the task at hand. Clarity on this is essential if an organization is going to align its decisions and resources toward success. So if you want to rule out identity as an issue that blocks your efforts to create a great workplace, the first question to ask yourself is Do you and your team understand the mission, vision, and values of your organization?

The *mission* defines the fundamental purpose of the organization—its reason for being. At Nike, a best company to work for, the mission is "to bring inspiration to every athlete in the world." They go on to note: "If you have a body, you are an athlete." The mission is a clear, memorable statement that defines

49

the purpose of the organization for all stakeholders—both internal and external. Bill George, the former CEO of Medtronic and a board member of Goldman Sachs (both best companies) observed in a *strategy + business* interview, "The leader's job today, in twenty-first-century terms, is not about gaining followership. Followership is an outmoded notion. Leadership starts with gaining alignment with the mission and values of the organization: What are we about? What do we believe as a group?"[2]

You will note that an effective organizational purpose doesn't have much to say about "increase shareholder value." Certainly, a requirement of a for-profit is to return value to its shareholders, but we find most often that mission articulates what the firm's purpose is in the world. While not all organizations that are best companies have identified distinct "mission statements," they all have clearly articulated reasons for existing. For example, Zappos aims to "provide the best customer service possible," and Whole Foods Market aims to operate in accordance with a "Declaration of Interdependence." Accordingly, the first question you may ask when getting clear about identity is What is your organization's stated purpose and what does that mean in terms of you and your team's responsibilities?

The *vision* of an organization is its long-term view of the future—a possible future that serves as a north star for everyone's work within the organization. As an example, a charity that supports basic nutrition for people might have the vision of "a world without hunger." A vision can articulate both quantitative as well as qualitative aspirations for the future of the organization. While an effective vision tends to be inspirational, even the most mundane statements work, as long as they helps everyone understand where they are going over the long term. This allows employees and other stakeholders to understand the overall direction of the organization, and in many cases is a springboard for finding meaning in their work.

The *values* of an organization are the basic rules or tenets by which the members of the organization agree to behave. Values drive an organization's culture and priorities and provide a framework in which decisions are made. Because it is such an important driver of culture and behavior, we often look to statements of values when first introduced to an organization. And, if the leaders cannot produce a set of values, or if they dismiss them as soon as they hand them over, that tells us something about the organization's identity as well—it's fragmented!

The Coca-Cola Company notes that their values act as "a compass for [their] actions and describe how [they] will behave in the world." Their values (abbreviated below) include

- Leadership: The courage to shape a better future
- Collaboration: Leverage collective genius
- Integrity: Be real
- Accountability: If it is to be, it's up to me
- Passion: Committed in heart and mind
- Diversity: As inclusive as our brands
- Quality: What we do, we do well

Managers and employees at The Coca-Cola Company talk frequently about their values and how these are expressed in their daily activities, and because their values are so ingrained, they do so without even realizing it. One of the managers we interviewed told us this story: "There was a guy I worked with who wasn't feeling engaged until he got involved with forming an internal company chapter of an international professional organization. Now, he has won several awards, built the organization's presence within The Coca-Cola Company, built external college chapters, and The Coca-Cola Company is getting the credit because they bring people inside the company to have meetings. The associate's passion for the brand has paid off for him and the company."

Your organization's values are unique, and we may not hear employees using the word "passion" in your organization. But the important point is to understand your values and how they shape the very way your employees interpret organizational events.

We find that a big challenge for some organizations is to "live the values." When an organization lives by two sets of values—a set of values that are expressed and another that are observed—then the mixed message can result in unintended consequences. For example, we once worked with a company that had a core value of "we interact with each other in a way that is respectful, fully transparent, and fair" and yet managers were asked to not discuss the company's strategy with employees. Employees became very cynical over time, and did not trust that information they received was "fully transparent." This ultimately resulted in low trust, low engagement, and low performance.

Organizations tend to invest a lot of time and energy into creating different workplace policies and practices to support their values and the workplace. Sometimes those policies are world class and cutting edge, such as those that we see at the listed best companies. And sometimes they are not world class, but they do resonate for the leaders and employees in the organization. They fit the organizational identity and context, and that is what is important.

The first task of understanding and aligning to your organization's identity is to examine your organization's mission, vision, and values. If your organization has these elements already, then find a way to interpret them for your own work group in a meaningful way. If your firm doesn't have all of these elements, then you should create something that will help your own team find their footing. We once coached a manager who had difficulty translating the organization's mission into something meaningful that could resonate for him. Their mission was to "work with stakeholders to advance modern chemicals," and it seemed, to his thinking, fairly generic and not very inspirational. We found that by considering the second- and third-order reasons for the company's products in the world, it became clear that they have a real impact on mitigating hunger, and that his team was instrumental in ensuring that the products had wide and timely distribution. He suddenly had new language and a new way to understand how he and his team aligned to the organization's mission and vision. And, even if his organizational leaders didn't communicate it in those terms, he could do so in his own work group.

If you find that your organization has a generic mission statement that your team doesn't connect to, dig deeper. Sometimes it is useful to consider the broader reasons for your products or services in the world. What purpose do they serve? Who benefits? How do your products or services impact the community, people's health, the environment, etc.? And what is your team's specific role in getting such products or services out into the world? Getting clear on your firm's mission and vision can go a long way to creating a solid organizational identity.

Strategy

> I have always thought that one man of tolerable abilities may work great changes, and accomplish great affairs among mankind, if he first forms a good plan, and, cutting off all amusements or other employments that would divert his attention, make the execution of that same plan his sole study and business.
>
> —*Benjamin Franklin*

While we do not believe that you need to cut off all amusements and we do believe that women can work great changes too, Franklin's sentiment about the value of a having a good plan is sound wisdom. We find that best companies have created a strategy for winning in the marketplace. They understand at a very deep level what they are there to do as an organization, and they also know that successful leaders are more likely to be trusted.

We usually frame the idea of a great workplace from the perspective of employees, but we can flip it to be more relevant to the manager role as well. As Great Place to Work® Institute co-founder, Robert Levering, highlights, a great workplace from a manager's point of view is one where you achieve your organizational objectives, with employees who give their best, all in a team or family environment. Achieving organizational objectives is first, and you will articulate them as part of your strategy or plan. It identifies how you will meet the needs of your target market, with the right products or services, and differentiate yourself from the competition.

While simply having a plan helps you articulate and act from an organizational identity, involving people in your plan helps to embed that sense of identity while also building the trust found in great workplaces. Linda Donlin from Mayo Clinic observed, "I think that when we made the decision to share the strategic plan with all employees, it was an easy decision to make because the leaders who shaped the plan looked at the values first and included that in how the plan was created and why we're doing the things we're doing. We re-communicated the values and then communicated the future direction. We talked very frankly about some of the challenges we faced in the world around us and talked very transparently about what the plan was going to be and encouraged employees to submit ideas or ask questions about the plan." At Mayo, as in your organization, the values are the touchstone for both the content of the plan and your approach for developing it.

There are a lot of resources to help companies create a clear strategic plan, and while our purpose is not to lay out a step-by-step process here, we would offer that effective plans: 1) provide a clear road map for achieving the firm's goals; 2) involve as many stakeholder groups—including employees—as possible; and 3) are deeply understood and shared by the organization. If you want a winning business, you need to start with a winning strategy and ensure that leaders across the organization understand and share in that strategy.

Sometimes the organization's strategy is not fully disclosed to all employees for a variety of reasons, including complexity, security (in government and military organizations), competition, and preparations for mergers and acquisitions. If this is the case with you, it is still important to examine and understand how you and your team's work advances the organization, and how it syncs with tangible, concrete outcomes for the business. The leader of the distribution group at one company we worked with shared with us that he takes the financial information shared at the Quarterly Town Hall meetings, and translates that into pallets shipped, because that is a unit of production that his employees understand far better than profit margin. Team members are immediately connected to the greater work of the company. If you don't have full visibility into the organization's strategy, find a useful link to connect with how your team's work supports the whole.

Management Structure

A winning strategy, however, will not suffice on its own. Best companies have also identified the management system that will best support them in their efforts. This includes the business model, structure, and processes that support the mission and vision and can deliver on the strategy. Best companies invest a lot of time thinking through the critical aspects of their business architecture and deploying them in the organization.

Some best companies have very flat organizational hier-archies, where others have multiple levels and layers. Some companies foster a collaborative, team approach, where others reward individual contribution and excellence with advancement in a hierarchical structure. Some of these organizations are pro-fessional service firms where the supply chain is limited to the office where the employees show up to work every day, and other firms have supply chains that extend around the globe. Manage-ment structure follows strategy.

The Coca-Cola Company operates as a franchise organization and global supply chain in over 200 countries around the world. Whole Foods Market operates 340 stores around the U.S. and sources its fresh, all-natural produce from local and global sources. Zappos is an online retailer where customer service is job one, and they have developed a state-of-the-art system and employee team to respond to customers. These companies' structures differ greatly, and they are all great workplaces. Above all, it is important to have a management system in your organization that makes sense given the mission, vision, values, and strategy. Doing so not only allows for operational efficiency in accomplishing your goals, but it reinforces the sense of organizational identity.

While you may or may not have a lot of direct influence and impact on the overall organizational architecture, how you work with your business objectives and creating a great workplace culture is within your control. At The Coca-Cola Company, for example, managers use the complexity and global nature of their supply chain as an important cornerstone for how they build their teams. Managers want global, diverse, and experienced teams to address the many challenges and opportunities that arise. In other words, teams are structured to reflect and capitalize on complexity and globalization, not to work around it. One manager offered, "I work with a team that is very virtual and very far apart. [My focus becomes about helping them] find the different mediums to understand what's happening and the challenges they face, and helping them to stay connected to one another." She went onto note that building on these aspects helps make a "big difference in keeping them engaged and inspired."

Workplace Culture

> Five frogs are sitting on a log. Four decide to jump off. How many are left? Answer: five. Why? Because there's a difference between deciding and doing
> —*Mark L. Feldman & Michael F. Spratt*

Workplace culture is the collection of policies, programs, and practices that guide the assumptions, behaviors, and habits of employees. It includes such things as working language, symbols, and habits. Culture, then, is less about what is formally stated or decided; instead, it shapes how people actually behave (like the frogs in our quote above). In your company, do people live by the rule "if you are on time, you're late" or "we will start the meeting at 9-ish"? That and a lot of other ways of working and working together are all signs of organizational culture. There is no one "right" workplace culture, as we wrote in *The Great Workplace*, but all great workplace cultures are strong.

Dan Warmenhoven, former CEO of NetApp, said it very elegantly when he noted that culture is values plus behavior. We'd extend that to say that culture is values, strategy, and structure, in addition to all of the activities that make those plans come alive. The mission, vision, and strategic plan provide the direction, and the management structure and values provide the alignment. Culture is the sum total of behaviors that are enabled by structure and alignment.

In a way, culture and organizational identity are one and the same, but like our personal identities, it helps to have signposts to make identity easier to talk about and act from. For instance, your identity is comprised of your credentials, goals, and roles, but also your personal assumptions and beliefs. Having a strong sense of personal identity helps you explain your perspective to others, and to consider opportunities and choices deliberately.

With regard to culture as an aspect of organizational identity, those signposts are more elusive. While you can identify your own assumptions and beliefs, it is more difficult to determine the assumptions and beliefs of an entire system, like a work group or organization. However, it is possible to do so by paying attention to artifacts, or visible evidence of the assumptions at work. Consider how people dress, the regular work hours, how managers interact with employees, and how friendly employees are with each other. Do managers stay in their offices? Do they sit with employees? Do they walk around or do they expect employees to come visit them? All of these point to how the culture operates. Look for these signs in your own organization, and fold them into your understanding of organizational identity. Failing to do so sets you up for excuses, because you will either be paralyzed when determining what behaviors will build the strongest relationships in your workplace, or you will fail miserably by unsystematically trying things that just might not fit.

A manager in the human resource department at Balfour Beatty Construction echoes this recommendation to understand your culture in order to create a great workplace. "Be crystal clear about the culture that you have, that you want to perpetuate. To me, there is no magic mix or profile of culture that is good for everybody. Goldman Sachs has been incredibly successful and they have a very hard-driving culture. Google has been very successful; they are very different from Goldman Sachs. Proctor and Gamble is different still. Bunch of nice people based in Cincinnati, but they are not Google and they are not Goldman Sachs.

So don't try to create someone else's culture. Just be real clear about what you want to be and who you are not."

It is important to note at this point that culture cannot be created. It is an outcome of several things, some of which are deliberate efforts to shape the culture, but more are the day-to-day decisions and behaviors in service of getting the work done. This is why, whether you are focusing on it or not, your workplace culture is what you end up with after you have implemented your strategy using the management systems that are in place. Culture will happen with or without you. One of the most common fallacies about culture we hear is that culture is different and distinct from the rest of the business. "Culture is soft stuff," they say. "We need to focus on the real business." It is as if they believe they can engage in the normal operations of the business while staying culture-neutral. Of course, you can't. Your culture is *how* you do your business. Therefore, it is important to understand that every organization already has a culture, and you simply cannot change or swap out cultures without examining the strategy and structure of the firm.

Organizational identity is made up of these various components and how they interact with each other. In great companies, they reinforce and support each other. A clear mission and vision is supported by values that are shared and lived. The management system aligns well with the business strategy to support an efficient work process. A clear understanding of the strategy and guidance from core values gives rise to a workplace culture that supports the mission and vision. All of these things work together.

UNDERSTANDING AND ALIGNMENT

We know, of course, that everything we've said in this chapter is easier said than done. We sometimes refer to mid-level managers as the "sponge layer" of an organization. Demands, needs, and communication are channeled to managers from their teams, from executives, from clients and other external stakeholders—from everywhere—and managers end up taking in all of that. But like sponges, they can only hold so much before water (or work) leaks out. When managers take in excessive information, it becomes challenging to determine exactly where they should focus their energy and attention, let alone to what they should align their efforts.

We have worked with clients where managers were unclear as to the organization's mission. In one organization, we asked three managers what the mission was and what was the most important organizational goal, and we received three different answers—even though the organization had a well-documented strategic plan. We were told that the values were "in the employee handbook," but those values were disconnected from how people acted or how people were incentivized. Managers indicated that because of "all the changes" and "ambiguous goals," it was best to just play it safe and slow and wait things out. These excuses for inaction masked the deeper issue at hand: lack of understanding of the organization's identity.

Another company we consulted with had a fairly strong sense of their mission, values, system, products, and culture, but there was a systemic problem in how people were hired, developed, and rewarded. For example, none of the questions in the hiring process examined an applicant's flexibility and ability to deal with ambiguity, although that was an important characteristic of the most successful employees. In other words, people who were hired were a mismatch for the company's culture. The result was poor alignment and negligible execution on the company's goals. This should hardly be surprising. In their book, *The Leadership Challenge*, authors James Kouzes and Barry Posner[3] note that high commitment is most evident when there is both clarity about the organization's values *and* coherence with one's own values. However, in this example, though the managers had coherent personal values, they couldn't do much without clarity about those of the organization.

The unfortunate issue with these clients was that they, in fact, had most of the basic building blocks. You can't be in business for very long without a sense of direction, a plan, and an approach to how you will deliver your products and services. Most organizations we work with have a strategic plan, a vision or mission statement, codified values, and a management system for getting the work done. The challenge lies in how effectively and completely managers *understand* and are *aligned* to those building blocks.

From our vantage point, if a manager has low understanding and alignment with the organization's identity, then it becomes really tough to move forward. And if a manager cannot see a clear path for success—even if there actually is one—then the likelihood for excuses or rationales will increase. Therefore, the clearest way to not fall into the trap of making such excuses is to have a clear sense of the organization's identity. We find that in organizations where managers "know the organization," they can act more freely and engage with employees, customers, and other stakeholders in a more confident, clear manner.

The most useful strategy, therefore, to address the challenge of "taking on too much water" is to have a deep understanding of your firm's identity. It is important to understand you have agency, and by this we mean the ability to act. Therefore, the more you understand the common elements of an organization's identity, the more you can act from solid ground. It will give you greater range from which to respond because your core is solid. Creating a great workplace begins with the right approach and the right information. Let understanding your organization's identity provide you with the tools to leverage that information as a strength in creating a great workplace. However, effectively acting

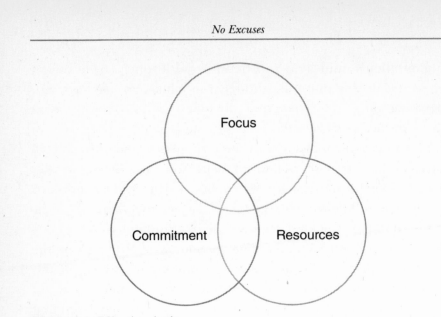

Figure 3.1 Effective Action

from a place of identity rests upon three fundamentals: focus, commitment, and resources.

FOCUS, COMMITMENT, AND RESOURCES

Having addressed the challenges of putting the basic building blocks in place, the other key challenge for leaders at all levels is ensuring effective action, as shown in Figure 3.1. We find that actions that achieve organizational objectives are greatly enhanced by having the appropriate focus, commitment, or resources for the task at hand.

In Bruch and Ghoshal's excellent article, "Beware the Busy Manager,"[4] they note that fully 90 percent of managers they studied over a ten-year period of time squandered their time in all sorts of ineffective activities. A mere 10 percent of managers spent their time in a committed, purposeful, and reflective manner. What separates the 10 percent from the 90 percent? They suggest "focus" and "energy" are the driving forces. In our experience, we believe that "energy" combines both commitment and resources.

Effective leaders *focus* their energies and efforts on specific goals and projects. They identify the vital few things that they will attend to, and those things are logical outgrowths of identity. Certainly, the reality of life as a manager is that there always seem to be more things to address than one has time for, yet we find really effective managers have found ways to address the "important and not urgent" before the "not important and seemingly urgent." They work hard not to get side-tracked.

Effective action also requires that leaders ensure *commitment* to the organizational objective or project. Ensuring that you and team members believe in the project and understand how you "plug in" or what your role is in the project is essential. One client we worked with had a project that was barely making progress. We soon discovered that the team's leader did not believe in the project, and most of the team members did not know what their roles were. There was no commitment to actually getting the project completed!

Finally, the right *resources* are needed to actually move the project forward. Resources may be financial, human, physical/material, or intangible (such as intellectual property or brands). No organization works with unlimited resources—there are always resource constraints; however, the resources need to be appropriate to the task at hand in order to make measurable progress. And effective leaders need to think through how to manage resource tradeoffs, such as the tradeoff between the need for expediency on the one hand and the available people power to bring the project to completion on the other.

As the Venn diagram Figure 3.1 suggests, leaders need all three aspects—focus, commitment, and resources—to achieve effective action. If you have the right commitment and appropriate

63

resources, but no focus, the effort becomes diffuse. If you have the right commitment and focus, but no resources, the project will never leave the starting point. And if you have the appropriate resources and right focus but no commitment, the project will suffer from lack of enthusiasm and engagement.

As a leader, you have a lot of opportunity to create a great workplace that leverages the talent and energy of your people in service of your company's organizational objectives. The first step is to reframe how you think about the work of creating a great workplace. And the second step is to understand your organization's identity, and either build upon it or reinforce it within your own work group so that you can use it in service of creating a great workplace. Working through such issues as mission, strategy, and values provides a clearer line of sight as to what you need to do to help your team win. And having the right focus, commitment, and resources will ensure that you are able to execute on organizational objectives.

CHAPTER 4

I DIDN'T HAVE ENOUGH TIME TO DO IT RIGHT

As we discussed in Chapter 2, there are several cognitive obstacles that get in the way of creating a great workplace. There are also behavioral obstacles that keep us stuck. In later chapters of the book, we'll talk about obstacles specific to your leaders or coworkers, or the very systems in which your organization exists. As all good philosophers say, you need to start with you and your own management behavior. Or as Yoda in *Star Wars* said, "Try not. Do or do not. . . . There is no try."

How many times have you protested, either verbally or mentally, that you just can't get in the habit of doing something you know is good for you? How frequently do you have conversations about the lack of time available to do new things during your work week? How about commiserating with others about false starts—your own or those of your work group? And, when all of those explanations fail to give you the satisfying feeling of being off the hook, perhaps you say things like, "Being *that* kind of great manager . . . it's just not me." All of these little surrenders are perfectly normal when faced with work that is important and effortful, even when you passionately believe in the outcome that exists on the other side of that effort.

One of us is often heard saying, "All this talk of wild success makes me want to go lie down." Of course, it is meant to be ironic . . . snarky even. But there's a truth to it. You may know by now, almost instinctively, that a great workplace is attainable with your hard work. You may delight in the very thought of it. But that sense of possibility and accomplishment does not come without cost. It is often accompanied by the visceral understanding that along with hard work and effort come exhaustion, rejection, failure, embarrassment, and uncertainty. It's no wonder that we allow our excuses to get in the way of even so much as taking the first step!

In this chapter, we discuss three of the behavioral excuses we hear most often: lack of time, energy, and skills. At the end of the day, human habit drives all of them. It shouldn't go without saying that great workplace managers are human too, and subject to all of the same behavioral traps you are. They find a way to defy them, though, and so can you.

TIME

No manager that we've ever met talks about having an abundance of time. Time is always at a premium, in some organizations even more than financial resources. Research confirms our experience with managers, and the statistics paint an even bleaker picture. According to a study by the Family and Work Institute released in 2012, and summarized by Karen Leland, 89 percent of American employees believe they never have enough time to get everything done, and 36 percent said they weren't planning to take their full allotment of vacation days.[1] In what may seem to be a cruel paradox, the investment of time it may take to shift habits and implement great workplace routines means further taxing employees' sense of accomplishment, let alone their time to take vacations and recuperate.

Pressures are even worse for managers with goals of career advancement. Hewlett and Luce noted in 2006 that "even the 60-hour workweek, once the path to the top, is now practically considered part-time, as a recent *FORTUNE* magazine article put it. Our data reveal that 62 percent of high-earning individuals work more than 50 hours a week, 35 percent work more than 60 hours a week, and 10 percent work more than 80 hours a week."[2] If you are working this much already, no wonder it seems as if the "one more thing" of creating a great workplace is too much.

Given the pressure to spend more time on work that leads to career success, and the sheer number of people in the work environment who feel overwhelmed with their current workload, it makes sense that managers would cite the lack of time as an excuse. The self-examination needed to change behavior does take time, and we sympathize with managers who tell us that it is easier to do things the way they've always been done. But we find there are a few simple rules and perspectives that help managers create a great workplace efficiently.

Change *How*, Not *What*

First, resist the temptation to create your great workplace by taking a brand new approach. Instead, change *how* you do what you already do. Going back to the idea that workplaces become great ones when employees feel a sense of trust, pride, and camaraderie, your work is to strengthen those perceptions. Many times you can do that without rolling out a whole new department-wide policy or practice. While any behavior shift will require a bit of time to override past habits and reward new behaviors, your first steps to a better workplace shouldn't feel like they take an inordinate amount of time.

To illustrate, consider these common managerial shifts. Chances are, you pause your work to eat lunch . . . at least once in a while. Perhaps you can dedicate one day per week to eating lunch in the break room, where you can have conversations with employees in your work group. It increases your approachability, because people get to know you as a person (rather than only their manager). And it allows people to ask the type of questions that help increase their understanding of how they contribute to your organization's mission, strategic direction, and near-term goals.

Encouraging more collaboration doesn't have to mean systems and channels for doing so beyond those that you already have at your disposal. What about dedicating the last ten minutes of each staff meeting to an open forum about a specific topic, client challenge, or process improvement? The conversations that start in those meetings may lead to more informal conversations later, and they may signal that you are open to suggestions and recommendations, both of which contribute to your employees' feelings that you respect them.

Even shifting focus in meetings to acknowledge successes can change the environment in meaningful ways. One Whole Foods Market team leader told us that taking the time to celebrate in meetings helps everyone feel more appreciated: "At a previous job of mine, in our meetings, it was literally said that it was not a time to talk about what we've done right, but that it was a time to talk about what we need to change. It was a culture of fear and negativity. Here, every part of our meeting is about appreciation. It's not fake; it's not forced. We genuinely appreciate what somebody else has done and you walk away feeling good." While it may not be the case that every aspect of your meetings is appreciative, taking the small bit of time to thank people for things relevant to the content of the meeting is worth it.

Helping people feel full members of the organization can be accomplished through language, which ultimately costs only the time it takes to remember to use one term where you previously used another. At Marriott, employees who work behind the scenes in the kitchen, or who come to work in the wee hours to set up for events, are said to work in "the heart of the house," rather than "the back of the house." At Zappos, job titles are unique and quirky, which helps people to feel their work makes a difference. There, you will find the Director of Casual Lifestyle, the Clothing Czar, the Love Bug, and the Happiness Hippie.

See Time as a Critical Investment

The point here is to illustrate several ways in which you can take steps toward a great workplace without spending a lot of time, but we'd be remiss if we didn't also suggest that investing time in people creates payoffs in productivity and loyalty down the road. At Teach for America, where they are experiencing rapid growth and ever-increasing geographic dispersion, they invest time in a centralized, in-person orientation program. As Aimee Eubanks Davis, Executive Vice President, People, Community and Diversity, told us, "We decided to bring people together for new hire orientation in order to ensure that there were very consistent messages being delivered. That was really critical for us and I think that's critical for [what ultimately is] a virtual work environment. To be frank, a year ago, we thought that we could potentially make new hire orientation virtual as well, but it was a complete disaster. Now, we understand that it's critical to our culture to bring people together within their first 90 days to hear about who we are, to engage in conversation, and to make sure people are connected to each other."

69

At the manager level, one-on-one meetings, time dedicated to celebrating success, post-mortem meetings to help make processes run more smoothly all take time. But the trusting relationships built with managers and fellow employees, not to mention the information exchanged in these forums, can be a boon to productivity and efficiency. At Whole Foods Market, they use team members in the hiring process, which is an investment of employees' time. But as their leaders will tell you, taking team members off the floor means better hires and a stronger commitment to the new employee. One leader told us, "At a lot of companies, you have one person who does interviews and then you bring this new person onto the team and no one else that they're working with has any experience with them at all. Here, we do group interviews. We involve people in the decision-making process on who's going to be hired. When they come on the team the first day, they've already met a lot of the team and the people who have interviewed them have ownership in helping them succeed."

Prioritize

Another way to help ease the burden of time for yourself and your employees is to get clear on priorities. While many things are important, only a few can be addressed at this moment, with the resources we have, in service to the ultimate goals of the organization. Implicitly and explicitly identifying those things helps to narrow your focus, and makes the priority of creating a great workplace more manageable. As we've discussed, culture matters to the success of the organization. Great workplace leaders back us up on that, many going so far as to say it is every manager's first priority.

Walter Robb, Co-CEO of Whole Foods Market, cited a show on Jim Cramer's CNBC show *Hospitality Index* as an illustration of how culture is becoming a legitimate fiscal priority. "[Kramer] did a show in the fall [of 2012] where he essentially said that when you want to evaluate companies for investment purposes, you need to look at culture. I called him up and I said, 'This is a watershed moment in American capitalism. You're a Goldman alumnus and you just told Wall Street to invest in the soft stuff.'"

A Zappos manager was even more pointed about getting priorities straight. She said, "I think if other people are saying they're too busy to think about culture, then what are they doing? That is a main function of our job. It's not necessarily something I consciously think about. I don't come in the door and say, 'Better manage that culture today!'" And yet, Zappos has an incredible culture. It is, in part, because managers know that their people are their priority. When that's the case, you don't have to "make time" for employees. Rather, creating a productive and positive workplace experience gets the lion's share of time, and everything else is secondary.

Last but not least, once you've made all the changes you can by changing how you do what you already do, made some investments, and gotten clear on priorities, you need to work hard to make sure the short-term pressures of the work environment don't pull you back into bad workplace habits. Sometimes, you need to simply say no in order to keep commitments, a hallmark of great workplaces. We asked leaders at Accenture, a consulting company known for its driven and achievement-oriented employees, how they manage the pressure to accept more work than they can reasonably deliver. Mary Edwards, a Client Account Executive, tells us, "I don't say yes unless I know I have time to do it. You can't say no to everything, but as many times as you say yes, you'll be asked to do more things. It's okay to say no in this environment. I've done it for six years and I've been incredibly successful." When we coach managers, we often remind them that their "yeses" mean more if they say no every now and again.

PERSISTENCE

Sometimes managers can find ways to use time smarter when it comes to their efforts to create a great workplace. But then they face an additional behavioral obstacle: a breakdown in persistence, or the energy needed to carry on building something as elusive as trust. We've all had the experience of seeming to "wake up" weeks after we successfully launched a process or shifted a behavior only to find that it has fallen by the wayside. It's not uncommon, particularly when we consider the amount of time needed to successfully adopt a new behavior.

Common wisdom has always suggested that behavior can only be changed if you execute on a new behavior for a period of two weeks, but in 2010, Lally and her colleagues found that habits take a longer period of time to form—an average of 66 days, but ranging up to 254 among her study participants for simple daily behaviors.[3] Given the number of priorities that managers often need to attend, maintaining a change in behavior over that time horizon is difficult. Managers need *symbols*, *rituals*, and *cues* to stay the course, and when we looked closely at companies we visited, we found them.

For Mayo Clinic, the shared passion for patient care mandates the collaborative and caring environment that their leaders create, and that environment serves as a *symbol* to remind people of their ultimate purpose. Dr. John Noseworthy, CEO of Mayo Clinic, told us, "Everything is about that. Why do we have gardens? Why do we invest in landscaping? It's for the patients. How would the patient feel if we didn't have the lawn mowed and people started to look sloppy at work? They wouldn't like that. Patient care trumps everything." He went on to tell us that when a tangible symbol isn't readily available, he sees it as part of his role to provide one. "If we're all physicians trying to solve a problem and we're all talking at each other, you just put something at the center of the table (like a water bottle) to symbolize the patient and to remind people when we're forgetting about the patient's needs. When we point to the symbol, people do two things. First, they get embarrassed, and then they relax and they remember that they're here to solve the problem for the patient and their family."

We coached a manager named Laura Brown who created a symbol for her medical records team—the "big cheese" award, named for the brass-plated wedge of Swiss cheese that traveled from desk to desk. While it was ultimately a way for peers to recognize one another for a job well done, it also served as a reminder to employees of something Laura said often: "All of us are a big deal to someone." Laura's staff has a huge impact on the lives of others in ways that they'll never directly learn about. When Laura first came to the team, no one seemed to realize their work mattered. Their error rates were abysmal, and turnover was high. By creating a symbol of employees' important role, Laura was better able to reinforce the behaviors she was trying to make habitual.

Rituals are another meaningful way to ensure persistence. If you know a recurring event will require you to perform, share results, or be evaluated for doing so, you are more likely to stay the course. Many managers we've worked with use regular one-on-one meetings as a mechanism to check in with employees about both their responsibilities and their experiences. Asking questions inviting feedback can be effective. For example, you may ask, "What is one thing you've experienced since we've last met that is positively contributing to your work experience?

Anything that is detracting from it?" That ritual, especially if repeated with some degree of frequency, ensures that you are always shaping the employee experience in ways that will elicit positive feedback. And, if your questions elicit negative feedback, you've still created open communication, which builds trust in the process.

One specific ritual may be to attend to data that is periodically available that may directly or indirectly serve as a feedback loop to your great workplace efforts. Turnover is a common example, though turnover data may not be as nuanced as it needs to be (turnover is often a function of many variables, only some of which are in your control). Those metrics that may be better cues are things like the number of times your people reward one another using a peer recognition system, or the attendance at brown bags and other informal events meant to build camaraderie.

Last but not least, *cues* can remind managers to attend to employee concerns. Fiat's Brazil plant has sign-in boards at the entrances of their plant with a traffic light graphic on it. When an employee comes in to work, they sign their name next to "where they are" that morning; green light if they are present and ready to go, next to the yellow light if they are present but not yet fully engaged, and next to the red light if something is going on for them—they are physically present but not mentally or emotionally present. Managers are responsible for reviewing the sign-in boards and pull people from their work stations if they have signed their name in the red area. They check in with them and see if there is something they can do to help the employee.

Of course, some people are better equipped to persist over long periods than others. Duckworth and her colleagues[4] call the manager's ability to overcome this obstacle "grit." More specifically, she says grit is perseverance and passion for long-term goals. Beyond decisiveness and creativity, managers must dedicate themselves to change in order to realize the results of their efforts. Interestingly, managers use personal characteristics (like grit . . . or the lack thereof) as a final excuse to avoid the behaviors necessary in creating a great workplace. They'll tell us that they just aren't people-oriented, or that they aren't good at inspiring others. And because personal characteristics seem static, defaulting to this excuse is often a final managerial surrender to the belief that it will never happen in their organization.

PERSONAL CHARACTERISTICS

All of us have strengths, and all of us have areas of opportunity. We have never met a manager who doesn't have the strengths needed to create a great workplace. Repeat: We have never met a manager who can't lead his or her organization in a way that builds trust, pride, and camaraderie.

Great workplaces are about relationships, and if you can build a relationship, you can create a great place to work. This truism is difficult for some managers to fully accept, and we see the reasons for their hesitation. Given the zeitgeist in the current leadership development realm that focuses us squarely on best practices and success stories as the best way to hone leadership skills, it is no wonder that we believe that most great workplace leaders are outspoken, gregarious and warm, optimistic, and cheerful. These leaders are comfortable conversing with small groups and speaking in front of large groups. They know everyone's name, they champion policies that are egalitarian, and they lead their organizations to success in the marketplace. No leader can live up to this, and believing that they can is counter to the very notion of a great workplace, where we focus on the how rather than the what. No matter what your skills are, how you use them is what creates a great workplace experience.

All of this focus on the prototypical great leader makes some managers conclude that their skills are woefully lacking. We have worked with countless managers who don't hold one-on-one meetings because they are "not touchy feely people," those who don't show appreciation because they are afraid it would come across as insincere, those who don't provide clear guidance because they aren't good with details—all are examples of managers who keep themselves (and their organizations) stuck. Could that same manager hold one-on-one meetings? Sure. Is it relatively easy to say "thank you"? Yes. Is it possible to provide details even though it seems pedantic to do so? Of course. Just as we spoke about in Chapter 2, the limiting belief is the first thing to address before changing behavior.

The next thing to do is to understand your own strengths. Try to adopt every best practice without doing so and you run the risk of becoming a "Frankenleader," as noted by Marcus Buckingham in his articles and talks about strengths-based leadership.[5] Frankenleaders are imitations of true leaders, people who inauthentically act as they think they "should" rather than deploying their own strengths to accomplish the same result. Inevitably, any attempt to reach a great workplace by adopting a Frankenleader approach will result in failure, because it relies upon the leader being someone he or she is not. Inauthentic leaders never have much luck in building trust with their work group, so you must find a way to lead from your strengths while making sure your strengths don't get in the way. If you are a data-driven leader, track the success-to-appreciation ratio and make sure it nears 1:1. If you are a creative manager, think of new and unexpected ways to bring fun to the workplace. You can often stay squarely in your comfort zone and do a fine job of creating a great workplace.

You can also move outside that comfort zone, and still produce the bottom-line results you may have been rewarded for to date.

The skills you use for doing so are not mutually exclusive to those that create a great workplace. We grant you that honing your skills in communication or collaboration may draw your attention temporarily from your current target. However, if you stay focused, you can develop skills that help you to build trust. Start with areas in which you already have some degree of strength, and repurpose those skills for trust building. Start small. Write one note of thanks per week, stop to say hello on your way to your desk, ask an employee for her feedback on an email—set yourself up for success by focusing on the behavior rather than the skill you believe you are lacking.

If you are in an organization that already boasts a strong culture, this may be easier for you. If you aren't in such an organization, make it your goal to create one. But first, you need to act. Let go of any self-limiting beliefs, identify your own strengths, and commit to behaviors you might use to facilitate a great workplace. We've met incredibly task-oriented leaders who are able to drive for results as second nature. They don't let go of that strength, and they don't apologize for it. Instead, they show appreciation for accomplishments and celebrate success with the same amount of determination that got them the results in the first place.

We've also met leaders who are not the most charismatic and skilled public speakers. They may be uncomfortable in the large group events that are necessary to their role, but they also make it a point to communicate in small groups in order to demonstrate their credibility. Some even write regular newsletters or blogs in order to ensure that people feel as though they know what their leaders are thinking.

We've encountered big-picture thinkers who empower their teams to create the schedules and coordinate resources; stalwart managers who lead teams by example, working shoulder to shoulder with employees in order to get the job done; and stoic realists who challenge their employees to help them think positively. In every manager is a set of strengths that can be used to build trust, pride, and camaraderie. Assuming your unique set of qualities does not lend itself to creating a great workplace is simply an excuse.

HABIT

Whether your excuse for not getting started is about time, energy, or skills, you are ultimately dealing with habits. Habits take time to change, and once they do, they persist indefinitely. Even a manager's reliance on a subset of skills can be considered a habit, and learning new skills involves the same process of changing routinized behavior. It is worth taking a minute to consider how to change workplace habits, because they are incredibly powerful. Even if we know what to do, we need to break through the very human process of autopilot—doing the same thing over and over because it takes less energy and involves less risk. The first thing we need to do in order to change habits is to realize they exist!

Habits have been studied in the fields of health, psychology, and consumer behavior for years, and recently they've garnered additional attention from neurologists. Habits, researchers find, are far beyond the particular repeated behavior that we know them to be. Rather, once a behavior has become a habit, it is precipitated by a complex set of cues.[6] In other words, when habits are at work, we behave in response to some multifaceted set of conditions that likely do not include our best intentions. We reach for a soda when we are faced with the cues of "exhaustion" and "only 2:00 P.M.," no matter our resolve to cut down on caffeine. We hit the snooze as a response to the alarm rather than getting up to work out, though we always feel better when we sacrifice the extra sleep for physical activity. We respond to environmental and emotional factors rather than cognitions and goals.

There is an additional complication involved in overcoming habits. They are so automatic that they are difficult to change after the cue-behavior sequence has been set in motion, regardless of intentions to behave otherwise. Once you realize you are simply repeating a habit, you are already doomed. Think of it this way: It takes a lot more energy to stop the ball from rolling down the hill once it is in motion than it does before it begins.

So how do you change your habits to be more in line with a great workplace? We draw on the appendix of Charles Duhigg's book *The Power of Habit* for some clues.[7] First, choose a habit you'd like to put into place. Perhaps you will stop and say hello to one team member on your way to your office every day. Or maybe you will make it a point in your communications to connect your decisions to organizational goals and objectives in order to help people see the big picture. Once you mentally commit to such behaviors, you may notice great opportunities to execute them . . . after the fact. Try to reward yourself for catching it, even if the opportunity to execute has passed. The moment you punish yourself for failing to execute, you set in motion the very cognitive obstacles we discussed in Chapter 2—you feel powerless to change, which we know isn't a productive pattern of thinking.

Next, identify cues that immediately precede the behavior. They should be cues that happen naturally in your work environment at the very same time you'd like to execute on your habit. For instance, maybe the cue to say hello to a team member is the keys to your office in your hand. Or, perhaps when you sit down to draft an email about a decision, you write the reasoning first to be sure it is there once you draft the details of the decision itself. Again, stay self-aware. Every time a cue happens, whether you execute on the habit or not, begin to link the cue and the behavior in your mind.

Last but not least, be sure to reward yourself. A reward can be as simple as reminding yourself that you are building a great workplace, interaction by interaction. Or, perhaps you'll keep a log of how often you keep your promise to yourself to execute on your habit. Even more tangibly, give yourself permission to get an afternoon latte once you reach a certain goal . . . and then offer to take a team member with you so you can rack up another point toward the next latte before you fully reward yourself for this one. Habits don't exist in the absence of some reward, even if the reward is simply the ability to tell yourself "Good job."

In this way, the cue will trigger the rewarded behavior over and over again until automaticity sets in. Then, you won't need to think about doing it, and any habit that wasn't creating a great workplace is elbowed out in favor of the new ones you create. We've talked with countless leaders about why they do what they do, or how they've gone about adopting behaviors that lead to a great workplace. As we discussed in Chapter 2, many of them fumble with the answer because their behaviors have become so automatic, and in many cases, have turned into organizational routines.

When groups of people respond to the same cues in the same way, we see an organizational-level habit, or what Geoffrey Hodgson, a researcher at University of Hertfordshire in the UK, calls a *routine*.[8] Hodgson notes that habits can be transmitted from person to person through incentive or imitation, both of which are key processes of organizational culture formation. In other words, the policies and procedures in your organization that guide behavior can create powerful routines, but so do the role models within the organization.

You are one of those role models, and accordingly, you wield power to create and sustain habits that you may not have known you have. Duhigg calls these "keystone habits," those transformative habits that, once adopted, spill over into every aspect of organizational life. Thus, the habits you have and create for others (through organizational structures or otherwise) do matter. Successfully change your management habits, and you'll change your workplace.

We saw this principle at work in an organization we visited where the manager adopted the cardinal rule of improv—Don't say no. Improv relies upon saying yes to whatever is in play, otherwise the scene stops. This manager took the same perspective in his approach to collaboration. "I just stopped saying no, banished it from my vocabulary. Early on, I would catch myself often, but I would always try to reverse it and instead say, 'Yes, and . . .' Over time, my work group began to think in more innovative ways, and I became more approachable in the process. Now, we try to get people to say no for sport. It's become that much of our culture." Simply changing his response to questions made his work group more open and innovative.

Sometimes, companies put routines in place for the sole purpose of investigating and changing counterproductive routines. At Zappos, the learning center does this to enable call center employees to perform better. One HR manager told us about "learning nuggets. If there's a trend on the floor that people are forgetting to put in call notes, we'll put together a training video that folks can watch." In this way, Zappos monitors trends and reverses them by training new cue-behavior sequences. For an example closer to workplace relationships, look no further than exit interviews to determine who is leaving and why. We've worked with more than one call center that has relaxed their discipline policies in response to losing good employees who arrive a few minutes late. The routine that had been put in place to require timeliness had an unintended consequence, so it needed to be changed. Routines are just habits repeated by a large group of people, and they can be changed in the same way: Investigate trends, identify the routines that give rise to them, and systematically replace them with a new routine.

WHAT TO DO NEXT

Given the behavioral obstacles to creating a great workplace, what might you do to overcome them? Though changing behavior seems like a short-term endeavor, it's not. Changing habits takes time, which is at a premium, and persistence can be difficult. And if you don't believe you have the skills needed to behave in new ways, that's one more reason to stay stuck. The important thing is to get started. Immediately, you can

- Recognize the very human tendency to behave automatically rather than in ways that are intentional and rational. Further note the cues and rewards surrounding your habits, your automatic behaviors, and begin to bring intention to the cues and the processes they set in motion.
- Write your intentions down. Research shows that committing to new habits in writing, particularly when those commitments focus on how to navigate those situations that are most likely to result in failure, leads to greater success in changing habits.
- Do something differently; don't just talk about doing something differently. It is virtually impossible to talk your way out of a situation you behaved your way into. Mary Edwards from Accenture puts it this way: "As a leader, you're a role model, whether you intend to be or not. You always have to be behaving consistent with the culture that you want to create. If you think it's important to have challenge in the environment, then your team needs to see you challenging your boss . . . and it being okay."

○ Reflect upon a few keystone habits, and put them into place in your organization such that they become routine. As leaders do at SC Johnson, hand out bonus checks personally and use them as a mechanism to show appreciation such that the entire work group ties organizational success to personal success. As leaders do at Mayo Clinic, set up reward systems that are tied to group performance in order to reinforce collaboration. Whatever environment you wish to create, there is likely a keystone habit or two that can ignite a larger culture change.

○ Acknowledge and reward others' efforts to break their habits. If you ask employees to be solution-based, focusing on ways to solve problems rather than simply presenting you with their concerns, show appreciation for their doing so, regardless of how feasible their solutions may be.

○ Infuse practices you already have with behaviors that build trust, pride, and camaraderie. Exhaust your opportunities to do so before putting a brand new practice into place.

○ Invest time in building relationships when possible. The payoff from doing so is a reduced need to spend time over-explaining decisions and convincing others to embrace risk, as leaders in low-trust relationships often find themselves doing.

○ Do fewer things well. Choosing to take on too much reduces the likelihood that you will succeed, and it may lead you to break trust in the process.

○ Identify and rely upon your strengths when it comes to specific ways in which you strengthen relationships in your work group. And if your development opportunities get in the way of doing so, figure out ways to manage around them.

CHAPTER 5

THAT'S JUST NOT MY JOB

One of the most consistent reasons we hear from managers as to why they cannot create or sustain a great workplace is simply because of their operating environment. Managers often share with us that they just don't believe they have enough time in the day to focus on their team. Sometimes they share that they are expected to focus their energy on other goals and initiatives that seem to have priority. Managers also say that the lack of budget or other realities are real impediments to effecting change. If you have ever thought that you face similar challenges, then you know what we're talking about. These are all facets of your firm's operating environment. And such challenges to creating a great workplace are omnipresent.

Perhaps your company's focus on short-term quarterly results make paying attention to any long-term opportunities—like cultivating high-trust relationships with employees—untenable. Maybe your HR department just isn't up to the task of being a supportive partner—or, conversely, HR is pretty much taking this on as their responsibility without providing the boots on the ground support you need. Or perhaps budget considerations—like a travel freeze—limit your ability to offer much support.

Whatever the particular reason, you believe that the current operating environment is at odds with the objective of creating a great workplace. You are not alone in your belief.

We find in our consulting work that most organizations today have a strategic priority of engaging their workforce. A 2012 study of CEO views of emerging trends and issues by IBM notes that more than 70 percent view empowering employees as a key strategic issue in firm competitiveness.[1] And yet, we also find that most managers feel a tension between "employees are an important asset" and "focus on firm results as your first, second, and third priority." This tension is really not an "either/or" problem, as we've already made the case for the correlation between empowered employees and firm results. But even if the goals are aligned on their face, they don't always feel that way—it can feel like strategic goals and operations goals are at odds, and so the dilemma about where to focus attention *is* indeed a very real challenge.

When we dig a little more into the "strategic-operations" dilemma, and we press managers to explain why the operating environment constrains them, they suggest four different reasons that their ability to focus time and attention on creating a great workplace is limited. First, they offer that the organization's goals and priorities hamper them—they are forced to wear too many hats. Second, they suggest there are limits on their role as a manager. Managers are rewarded for results, they say, not how much trust has developed.

The third reason managers see the operating environment as an obstacle is because they see someone or some other group as the party responsible for workplace culture. One manager shared with us that the "chief culture officer really owns this," which was his way of excusing himself. Finally, managers often share that even if they wanted to be more involved in creating a great workplace and did see it as their responsibility, they lack the power and authority to see it through. Decisions must go "up the chain" even for minor investments of time and energy that seem to deviate from core project goals.

All of these are understandable points of view, and likely, your experiences may be similar to those of many managers we work with. These reasons, however, still provide an easy excuse from engaging in the sometimes difficult, messy work of leading.

This chapter focuses on these four excuses, and how to keep them from getting in your way. We also explore the role of power and politics in organizations and its influence on how managers create and sustain a great work environment. Our hope is that you will really see "no excuse" for adeptly managing your organization's operating environment in service of creating a high-trust workplace.

MY GOALS AND PRIORITIES COMPETE TOO MUCH

Jane Adams manages an engineering department at a large electronics organization. The firm makes laptop computers, phones, and televisions. Jane has been working at the firm for over ten years, and started as an engineer out of college. She has a no-nonsense approach to managing people but understands well that business relationships are often complicated and not always straightforward. "I enjoy working with my team and when things are working well, we can move and adapt quickly. But their needs are each so different. What motivates one person does nothing for another."

Jane continues, "I often feel caught between my desire to understand what motivates them at work, and the expectations of our senior leadership to meet our goals. At the end of the day, what I am accountable for is ensuring that we meet our goals. If we don't, product delays occur, which can cost us millions." Jane is expressing a common concern that managers have in creating a great workplace. Even if the organization has a strategic priority on creating a great workplace, the demands of meeting financial goals and strategic priorities all at once can be overwhelming.

Sometimes it isn't the tension between workplace and business goals, but the goals themselves are unclear. Unclear goals readily lead to confusion, frustration, or disengagement and a ready-made reason to not focus on developing your workplace. One way to address this is to keep goals focused and simple. Remember that The Coca-Cola Company keeps its six-point strategy on one page. It allows it to be very clear and concise and to the point. It takes time and a lot of effort to make something like strategy and operational goals simple and concise. But the effort is worthwhile, as it helps with addressing the issue of goals being confusing or unclear.

Another common concern we hear from managers is that in today's dynamic environment, organizations are constantly shifting priorities or priorities are interrupted. Sometimes a pressing issue takes over the planned work of focusing on creating a great workplace. But there are solutions here, too, and shifting priorities need not be used as an excuse.

The best advice managers offer is to accept that shifting priorities happen. It's important to be flexible and adaptive. But this must also be married with close communication and collaboration with your team, and that advice is sound for all three of the goal-related excuses managers offer. If you navigate unclear and mercurial waters together, you can come out on the other side feeling either discombobulated and exhausted, or bonded and empowered. The difference between the two reactions lies in the strength of your communication.

At the best companies, managers go a long way to ensure understanding about how goals and people efforts are aligned, so that their managers don't face the problems Jane did about competing interests and priorities. As an example, Jill Smart at Accenture offered that "we ask something in our engagement survey about 'Do you understand how what you do is relevant to our strategy?' Our leaders are supposed to take our strategy and make it relevant to our people. Our people don't necessarily care if the specific job they're doing today is one of those ten priorities, but they want to understand how they contribute because, in some way, everybody is." Making the connections between strategy and employee contribution addresses the challenge of competing priorities in several ways. First, it reinforces the vital few objectives that need to be focused on by everyone. Second, it provides a way for managers and employees to make meaning of their work. And finally, it provides good "connection time" between employees and managers, which is vital in fostering workplace trust.

As a manager at The Coca-Cola Company explained, "[When I think about] 1987 versus today, we were much more focused on sales and marketing and right now, thanks to the strategic work that we carried on in the past eight to ten years [there is] a more holistic approach to business and life. We [now] know that everyone contributes to success." At The Coca-Cola Company, they took deliberate steps to put in place a strategy that includes a winning culture. And now, managers can draw upon this simple, straightforward, one-page plan to align efforts, better collaborate with team members, and support their ability to make a connection between their work and organizational outcomes.

That's how to emphasize alignment that already exists. But what if the aims of the organization actually aren't aligned with your attempts at creating a great work environment? The answer is actually simple: communicate. Communicate frequently, and communicate honestly. That very practice will still enhance trust.

A manager at Mayo Clinic shared how she did just that. "Open communication is a key thing. The other part is realizing that I don't have all the answers, and I say that very openly to my staff.

We can work together to figure out what we need to do if issues arise or people are out unexpectedly. We talk about it. And [it's not a] Pollyanna attitude, but it's a can-do attitude. We'll shift priorities and make time to do things. You figure out the game plan and get input from the people involved in it because they know what they can and cannot do. Then you work together to figure things out."

That turns out to be a very useful strategy because competing priorities, unclear priorities, or shifting priorities can frustrate employees and cause them to lose focus. At the Mayo Clinic, managers find ways to connect and communicate so that employees are constantly aware of what is going on in the organization. Another manager at Mayo offered, "Because we travel all over repairing machines, we usually start Monday with a meeting just over coffee. We talk about what's going on for the week; we talk about when we're free to help. Every Monday morning, all of my staff email each other with what they have planned for the week. We have a white board—which came about from an employee opinion survey because we were struggling with communication— that has the schedule for everyone for two months. If someone walks in and looks at the white board, they know exactly what's going on. That's been a huge satisfier to my staff—something as small as a $50 white board."

Jane took a similar approach at the electronics organization. She realized that she had some influence on how goals were cascaded throughout her team but very little control over the company's larger strategic goals, how priorities based on those goals were set, or why they shifted from time to time. But she was resolute in her desire to create a great workplace for her people— knowing that if she did so, she would be in a better position to meet the department's goals.

To do so, Jane followed an example from CarMax, a used-car retailer: making information accessible through a goal chart with traffic light–type markings for goal progress. For the high-level goals, she worked with the team to create action plans, and as a part of each action plan there was a focus on team learning and development. The goals were made visible for all to see and there was transparency into the progress toward goals attainment with the traffic light markings (green for "on target" versus red for "immediate attention"). Jane met briefly with her team each morning to review progress and discuss the very next step to be taken. Through this change in team interaction, she was also to simultaneously learn more about her team members' interests, needs, and work/life. By incorporating *how* she communicated and worked with her team, she was able to change the dynamic of competing priorities.

As a manager at Mayo offered to us, "We often have more priorities than are realistic. Like other organizations, we're always trying to get ahead of something. 'This is a great idea and we gotta do it.' We sometimes suffer from that. [So it is important to] use the values of teamwork and mutual respect [so that they're not viewed as] an add-on." Jane shared with us, "I can't control, the changes from above, but I can control what and how and how often I communicate with my team. And I figured that was the place to start."

BUT I CAN'T WEAR THAT MANY HATS

If you are like most managers, your plate is full. The role of the manager in today's organization has expanded beyond traditional notions of what is required. Beyond the planning, organizing, staffing, and managing that are typical characteristics of your role, you are coach, mentor, head negotiator, facilitator, teacher, and so on. You're balancing a rather complicated and tricky set of responsibilities.

The managerial role is critical in an organization's structure, and it follows that there's a great deal of research and business literature about managers' role and function, what constitutes effective management, and trends and issues in managing people. It's often said that people join companies but leave their managers, suggesting that—at the end of the day—it is your direct manager who has the biggest impact on your engagement and satisfaction. Similarly, your direct reports are constantly evaluating (albeit not always consciously) their relationship with you.

Not only do you have a sizable impact on how your team members think of the organization and their job, your influence also extends beyond them individually to their team members inside the organization and their families outside. If you think for a moment about the amount of time you spend thinking about work or talking about work—and about your managers and other leaders—outside of work, you know this to be true. Well, the same is true of the people you lead. In other words, your role matters. A lot.

Even as we are aware that we have a large influence on how our people experience their work and the organization, sometimes the role creates obstacles. In our work with managers, we find that the issue of "role" comes up in three different ways as a potential excuse for not engaging in the work of creating a great workplace. First, managers will often share with us that they are wearing "too many hats." Second, managers believe that creating a great workplace culture is outside of their role. And third, managers will sometimes confide in us that they don't know how to do it.

The role of the manager in today's organization is multifaceted to be sure. As a manager, you are juggling a lot of expectations and responsibilities. And if you have to prioritize, which parts of the role must you focus on? We sometimes hear from managers that while they are expected to create a great workplace, they are held accountable and rewarded for other facets of their role. They are "wearing too many hats" they say, and that if one has to "give" then it will be the role of culture creator.

Your role of creating a great workplace, however, should be your first priority. As a manager at NetApp offered, "Work product is what you work hard to do and you work long hours and weekends. But, when it comes down to the matter of managing a staff, I take that as a first priority. If there's an issue or if there's recognition that I have to give out, I take care of that first. The work stuff comes after that. It permeates through the organization. People see that as a priority and they start making it a priority for themselves." There are two important reasons to make this priority number one. First, is that by making people the first priority, it will shape all of your other priorities in a way more aligned with a great workplace. Another manager at NetApp suggested, "I go to great lengths to bring folks on my team who can benefit from the conversation I'm having. We have a lot of meetings, and I invite them. It's an opportunity to provide growth and learning for your staff. They can have a higher view of where they fit in. Managing while you work is beneficial."

The second reason is that by making this a key priority, it will help to address other managerial hats or supervisory challenges. In essence, as a manager you routinely communicate goals and objectives, make decisions, create plans and obtain buy-in for them, and empower people to go above and beyond. You need to do these things in the context of your role anyway. And when you have a high-trust workplace, your ability to do all of these things becomes easier and more efficient, as well as more effective. For example, in a high-trust environment, employees are more likely to ask questions and challenge assumptions, listen carefully, and when presented with a good plan, buy into that plan. Involvement of your team results in investment in the outcome.

Sometimes the issue regarding role is quite different than feeling like you have too many hats. For some managers we speak with, they believe that the task of creating a great workplace is *not* part of their role as a manager. They believe that their role is exclusively focused on managing the technical or business aspects of their team, and not the cultural component. The problem with this perspective, however, is that if you manage a *team*, you are responsible by default for creating a workplace culture that will support the team in meeting its targets and objectives. A team by its definition is a group of people focused on a specific task or goal, and if people are involved, then workplace culture comes with the territory. Better to effectively manage your team toward productive accomplishment of your goals than not address the aspect of workplace culture and risk suboptimal results on the team.

Perhaps the biggest challenge as it relates to your role as a manager is simply not knowing what to do! Managers we speak with in our consulting work confide that they often feel like they are "way out over their skis" on many people management issues. Most managers do not receive a lot of training before they take on the role (although that is changing somewhat). But even going through training or having access to "manager manuals" won't necessarily prepare you for the human relations challenges you will experience.

The first, biggest step you might take is to start with respect. As a manager at Mayo explains, "Even though you have all those things going on, it's not hard to start with respect for the employees who are in your department. There are things you can do to set the atmosphere regardless of the outside constraints you have. We're all dealing with a lot of those changes and integration and things, but at the end of the day, I don't think it has a tre-mendous impact on the environment that you set and the respect that you show and receive for those around you." As we have shared previously, treat every interaction as an opportunity to build trust.

Beyond the foundational building block, look for opportunities to connect with your team informally. As a manager at Mayo offers, "With my group, we are all managers, so it's busy. Once a quarter, we get together for coffee at Starbucks. We don't have an agenda, but it's our time to reconnect and talk about things both personally and professionally. I think those kinds of things can be done regardless [of budget]. It doesn't cost me anything to do that." Investing in the relationship can go a long way to building a great workplace, and it need not be an expensive proposition. The goal here is to think creatively and deeply about how to meet the needs of employees.

Finally, you may wish to use the Great Place to Work® Model© that we covered in the introduction of this book and discuss in detail in *The Great Workplace.* That previous work offers a range of case studies, stories, best practices, tips, and action items for you to enhance your knowledge about how to address workplace culture and manager dilemmas.

As much as the role of manager continues to expand beyond the traditional notions of what it means to "manage," there are real constraints on the role. This is understandable. But as the managers quoted earlier expressed, being aware and seizing opportunities to build trust, and finding the extra sixty seconds to engage with your people can make all the difference. It becomes less of an issue of *how much* than of *how.*

THIS IS SOMEONE ELSE'S PROBLEM

Let's talk about boundaries, by which we mean your responsibility versus my responsibility. One of the queries we often see in organizations facing the strategy/operations dilemma is "Who is responsible for creating a great workplace?" It's a legitimate question.

Human resources and its cousins, training and development and organizational development, are often the departments tasked with creating a great workplace in most organizations. This makes sense given they're seen as "people departments," and HR business partners devote much energy to supporting line managers. But in answer to who is responsible, the answer is *everyone*. Senior management has a responsibility, as do managers such as you. Human resources has a responsibility, and employees do, too. Yet that boundary or line between HR and your role as a manager gets a little muddy. Too often we see HR departments taking over the task of creating a great workplace, and managers and other leaders are ostensibly off the hook. Other times, we've witnessed ineffective HR departments that draft policy and manage the very tactical HR issues such as getting paychecks in the mail, but suffer from a lack of creativity, organization, and awareness of how to make a real impact.

You may be in an organization with a large HR department or an organization with no HR department. Your responsibility, really, is the same regardless of the size (or effectiveness) of your HR department. As a general rule in today's context, the first dedicated HR person comes in when the firm has around seventy-five employees. There's now more of a squeeze on HR; the ratios of HR staff to employees used to be 1:100, but now it can be more like 1:200 or 1:250. It's quite often the case today that key HR decision makers will hire an outside consultant for a one-shot project like creating an employee value proposition. We also see a trend toward outsourcing some of the more tactical and traditional HR issues like compensation and benefits. The point here is that HR cannot do it all alone, even if they wanted to.

Human resources, if you have such a department, can be a good partner to you in thinking through options and tools. But

96

at the end of the day, you will need to lead the effort. You cannot "throw it over the wall." As Ceree Eberly, the Chief People Officer at The Coca-Cola Company, shared, "Any strategy for creating the best workplace for our employees must be owned by business leaders. They must make it a business priority. It has to matter to them, or the strategy will not work. HR's role is to support and enable the strategy by leading the process, but it will be a flawed strategy if HR owns it."

A joint study by the *Economist* newspaper and consulting firm KPMG[2] found that only 17 percent of executives believe their HR departments to be effective, and many also see their HR department as non-essential. The best-case scenario is that this is a perception problem, but it also stands that many leaders actually find their HR departments wanting in terms of strategic guidance when it comes to human capital. If you perceive your HR department as ineffective, what can you do to create a great workplace?

It turns out that you can do a lot in the absence of an effective HR department. You can support your people through active communication and collaboration, hiring employees who are good culture fits, thanking people for a job well done, celebrating special events and successes, and finding opportunities to support them in their career or professional development. Scores of tools and books—including our previous title—exist on how to do so. Don't say it's someone else's job—it's not, and that's no excuse.

I DON'T HAVE THE POWER TO CREATE A GREAT WORKPLACE

The fourth common obstacle managers need to navigate in the operating environment is how authority and decision making are exercised. Authority is seen as the legitimate right of a person to exercise influence, make decisions, carry out actions, and to direct the efforts of others. Managers expect to have the authority to hire employees, assign work, organize teams, and manage performance. In creating a great workplace, two different obstacles tend to arise surrounding authority. First, managers experience that they have a lot of *responsibility*, but not the commensurate *authority*. This dilemma is usually related to expectations on managers by senior management or HR for creating a great workplace. (Another related issue is not feeling like you have the authority with your team because of issues like union contracts, which we'll deal with in Chapter 8.) The second obstacle surrounding authority is actually *exercising* that authority. Many managers we work with think that they need to be soft or indulgent with their team members, and that doing so is the route to a great workplace. Rather, holding people accountable is a marker of a great workplace.

Chris Johnson is a manager for a non-profit based in the mid-Atlantic region. As a manager in the development department, Chris has responsibility for major events and securing sponsors for the organization. The senior management team (of which he is not a member) has an explicit goal of becoming a great place to work. And the senior team has tasked managers like Chris with improving various people metrics, including their employee survey results. Chris shared that the senior management team has become less of a "senior management group" and more of a "senior manager's group." He notes that the senior team has gotten "in the weeds" with *how* managers across the organization are creating results, leaving managers like himself to feel micro-managed and disempowered. Says Chris, "I would like to have more of a voice in policy decisions. . . . I feel like there is a lot expected of me, but I'm not given the ability to enact policy or programs."

Chris' concerns are understandable, and he is not alone in thinking that he has been given a great deal of responsibility but not a lot of authority. Many managers often feel this way, but it is not a reason to avoid taking on the task of creating a great workplace. Most organizations develop policy and practices at the firm level. Managers initiate activities in their departments, although managers can also develop their own practices. We sat down with Chris and discussed what he was able to control, versus what he had influence over, versus what he had no control or influence over (but might be concerned about). In this case, it made more sense for Chris to focus on what he could change versus what he couldn't. And what we discovered was that there was a lot that Chris could do.

Chris had been with the organization for over seven years, and his tenure, coupled with his particular job, gave him quite a bit of influence with the director of development and the executive director of the organization. He just hadn't considered what influence he had and how to use it. Chris created a case study and presented it to the two directors to articulate the problem of manager inclusion and ways to bring their perspective into the culture conversation. The second focus was to work with his colleagues on areas of mutual purpose and concern. With multiple parties involved, Chris was able to accomplish more (such as a monthly recognition program for employees in development). And third, Chris was able to remove some barriers to effective action. For example, by inviting senior managers into team meetings more frequently, he was able to have senior managers demonstrate their commitment to creating a great workplace by actively listening to employees.

As a manager, you actually have a great deal of authority, whether or not it's apparent. You can influence, communicate, raise questions of accountability, and use aspects of the organization's identity—such as its values or strategy—to move an agenda forward. Perhaps the bigger challenge is actually using the authority you have to make decisions and implement change.

Becoming comfortable with exercising authority is one of the hardest tasks for most managers, but it's also one of the most important if you want to be effective. Authority is based on your position, although it is often viewed as arising from interpersonal relationships too. And that is where most of the concerns arise. We once worked with a manager, Susan, who tried everything to move a program forward with her team—pleading, cajoling, guilt-tripping—until we asked whether or not she had tried simply stating what she expected. After all, she was the boss. Susan held authority, but she wasn't using it.

Having clear expectations for what is appropriate, setting goals and standards, and articulating and enforcing consequences are part of the responsibility and authority of being a manager. Of course, it's good to foster a supportive relationship with employees, but at the end of the day, you will still be held accountable for results, and so you need to hold employees accountable for *their* results. Susan's difficulty exercising authority fell on the opposite end of the continuum than the operational challenge we cited surrounding goals. With the latter, the manager's focus is squarely on the results to the detriment of the relationships. With managers like Susan, the focus is squarely on the relationship to the detriment of results. Having a great workplace means focusing on both, and enjoying the way they come together.

Authority is sometimes equated with legitimate power. How authority and power relate is vital to your effectiveness as a manager. When your team perceives your use of power as legitimate (or honest or good), then they are more likely to see it in its appropriate light and comply. How power is used in an organization is the subject of the next section.

ORGANIZATIONAL POLITICS

If you think about the word "politics," negative images are likely to come to mind. Most people have an adverse reaction to the idea of politics. It conjures ideas of warring factions pushing their own self interests. We use phrases such as "politicking," "playing politics," and "it was just political" with a negative connotation.

Power is a key element in understanding politics. Power stems from a variety of sources, including reward power, coercive power, information power, resource power, expert power, referent power, and legitimate power. When people believe power is being purposefully used to guarantee some personal end, rather than one that serves the organization, they call that politics.

Thus, it is no small wonder that many of us are ambivalent about power. We understand its usefulness, but we would rather not talk about it. As Pfeffer observes, people are more concerned about the ends than the means, and therefore, they've trained themselves (and others) to avoid critical thinking and appreciation of how power can be used.[3] We often judge organizational decisions absent this understanding and appreciation of the influence of power, unless, of course, power was used negatively. Then, trust is broken, and we've lost yardage to a great workplace.

Better, then, to understand power and politics and how they exist alongside creating a great workplace. Bolman and Deal discuss the role of politics in organizations by sharing that "politics" is "the realistic process of making decisions and allocating resources in a context of scarcity and divergent interests."[4] Thus, there is an inherent political dimension to most decisions in every organization. But upon closer examination, there are also the threads of trust, particularly when you think of building trust laterally while building trust with your team.

As an example, we once worked with a manager who was angry at his team. A series of missteps and missed deadlines had created real stress on the team, and the manager had started to try and "teach them a lesson" by taking away flexibility and other benefits and instituting very tight controls. Unfortunately, the manager missed the opportunity to direct and coach the team. His efforts had the opposite effect of what he had hoped, as team members became even less engaged and productive. By (re)positioning trust at the center of his efforts, he was able to practice positive politics.

Allocating resources in service of the organization's identity is a good thing, as long as everyone involved remembers that all members of the organization are on the same team. As an example, efforts to bolster your organization's identity should be broadly inclusive (such as when a company is developing its operating plan). Considering divergent opinions and making decisions fairly are also remedies to the downside of politics. All organizations deal with scarcity; it is when decisions are made unilaterally that divide employees into the "haves" and "have nots" that we worry about the loss of trust.

Being aware of the antecedents of political decision making (i.e., decision making about scarce resources in a context of widely differing opinions), and dealing with them in ways that build trust rather than break it (like taking a broader perspective and hearing differing opinions) is your only choice. Of course, not everyone will treat those decisions in such a noble and thoughtful manner. But don't play into the "us versus them" archetype, either in your approach or your decisions.

It is important to realize, though, that regardless of your personal efforts, politics will still be at play some of the time. Believing they won't would be a naïve or overly simplistic view of how we build relationships. In great workplaces, managers build trust within the context of a political arena, but on the whole, they have high expectations for themselves. They try to avoid the pull to play along with the "us versus them" archetype, either in their approach or their decisions.

As a manager, you navigate this particular challenge by understanding the political context of your company, networking and building coalitions with others, and negotiating with others. This allows you to right-set expectations and clear the cognitive obstacles that might get in the way. To this end, Bolman and Deal[5] point out that the effective manager develops a set of skills to navigate the political terrain such as working to understand how communication flows in the organization or how to assess who might resist your attempts to influence. Many of these skills are basic to also creating a great workplace: being self-aware of your own needs and biases, communication, collaboration, and managing the change process.

The operating environment need not block your efforts at being an effective manager. Instead, a clear-eyed understanding of the operating environment, like your organization's identity, can help you identify useful ways of leveraging the talent of your team, create a more positive work atmosphere, and enhance the level of trust in the workplace.

In the next chapter, we'll turn our attention from the operating environment and how decisions are made or challenged, to the challenge of managing through or around our industry and marketplace's structure in order to create a high-trust, great workplace. Whether it is the nature of operating in a global organization, dealing with virtual teams, or the vicissitudes of your particular industry, these need not be barriers to creating a great workplace.

103

WHAT TO DO NEXT

When addressing the challenges of your operating environment and navigating the political dimension of your organization, it is useful to consider the following actions:

○ Think through how each person and every role contributes tangibly to organizational goals and outcomes.

○ Communicate to employees the significance and meaning of their contributions and provide regular feedback on this.

○ Look for opportunities to "close the loop" for employees between goals and their role; this helps to ensure alignment.

○ Identify all of the various "hats" you wear as a manager. Chart how much time you spend each week or each month "wearing" these various hats. What does this say about what you prioritize or what is demanded of you? How can you focus more energy in your role as a builder of workplace culture?

○ Consider what your commitment is to creating a great workplace environment, and what your unique role is in helping to create it.

○ Spend time considering what you have control over, what you have influence over, and those things that you are concerned about but have no control or influence over. Work within your circle of influence.

○ Spend time looking at how power and politics operates in your organization. Who has formal power? How has informal power? How are resources divided up or shared? Resources could be actually money but it could also be information.

CHAPTER 6

MY INDUSTRY IS DIFFERENT

While all challenges to a great workplace feel entrenched on some level, none seem more immovable than those that come from social, political, demographic, and market forces. Globalization, the health of the economy, demographic trends, environmental shifts, and shifting rules and regulations seem to restrict a leader's options, even as they provide opportunity for growth. Thus, megatrends such as these heavily (though not always observably) influence organizations and their leaders.

When the majority of organizations in the same industry respond to these pervasive forces in the same way, the excuses often show up at our consulting practice as *industry* excuses. It doesn't matter if the industry is manufacturing, professional service, healthcare, retail, or even education and government, as the excuses begin the same way: "My industry is different because . . ."

Some sub-industries also have unique workplace challenges as they respond to external forces. Company leaders in industries that have come under scrutiny, like banking and fast food, need to ensure that employees maintain a sense of pride in the mission while understanding and responding to criticism. Organizations with national brands that deliver their goods and services locally, like food and grocery and professional services, struggle with how to replicate culture across several locations and geographic demands. Companies that compete globally deal with replicating culture as well, although on a larger and more complex scale.

In this chapter, we will provide examples from a variety of industries, showing you how the best workplaces have met with these common external obstacles and cleverly moved them out of the way—or at least aside. But even as we hope they will give you ideas and inspiration, it's critical to remember a common, under-lying principle: *Every* decision—externally driven or not—is a people decision. And attending to the human impact in making any decision, including those that are in response to external forces or industry trends, is what makes a workplace great.

THE INDUSTRY NORMS EXCUSE

While every industry is truly different, many issues are not as unique as managers believe them to be. We've worked with man-agers in manufacturing or technical organizations that operated 24/7 who found they had much to learn from hospitals, where leaders also grapple with how to reach employees on night shifts. Colleges and universities, where faculty often have a dual alle-giance to their institution and their field of study, can take notes from high-tech organizations where innovation is often awarded with a patent for the individual scientist or engineer. Not-for-profit managers express concern for "doing more with less" and burnout, with which a remarkable number of mission-driven, for-profit companies also contend.

John Richels, President and CEO of Devon Energy, agrees that commonalities lay beneath the surface of seemingly different industries. "We're in the oil and gas business and I spent eighteen years in the law profession. There are a lot of similar cultural elements, even though it's a very different operating environment. What I've learned over time is that all of us are really after the same thing, no matter what business we're in. What we're looking for as employees and individuals is not specific to an industry. I think what people are looking for is a level of trust in the organization."

So while every industry *is* different, there is a collective wisdom from which we all can learn. In the pages that follow, we discuss the excuses we hear most often from professional service organizations, manufacturing industries, and not-for-profits. We hope you recognize a common thread that weaves through all of them. More importantly, we hope you can learn how to deal with challenges in your industry from companies in other industries, just as we have.

Professional Services: Work/Life Balance and Equity

Professional services firms are faced with pressures to remain constantly connected while on the go, decidedly blurring the lines between time that is considered on and off the job. Some would even say that there is *no* distinction in some companies. After all, the client's demands must be met in order to successfully compete. Last but not least, the hierarchies in professional services can create a collective sense of "have" and "have not" that is difficult to overcome. Specifically, when one group of employees is deemed as more essential to the business than others, efforts to build trust (and therefore a great workplace) through creating accessible communication, collaboration, and camaraderie fail.

The work/life balance challenge is one that intrigues leaders and researchers alike, perhaps because we all know what it feels like to straddle both worlds. When our kids text us during a meeting, or when our boss calls during the fourth quarter of the junior varsity basketball game, we can't help but be thankful that we are connected while also dealing with the annoyance of the intrusion. In a 2009 *Business Horizons* study that gathered data from 146 professionals across a variety of industries, the tension is summed up this way: "At first blush, the provision of connectivity would appear to equip managers and professionals with greater flexibility and, accordingly, help them juggle family and other life demands. However, gaining connectivity and flexibility was accompanied by feelings of increased responsibility, and both self- and other-imposed expectations and pressures to work more."[1]

Accenture deals with the constant demands and connectivity by being direct and unapologetic about the nature of the work, but also by offering support to its consultants as they meet the needs of the client. While the intensity of the work is a widely held perception of the consulting world, the needed support in some of the best firms is often overlooked. Jill Smart puts it this way: "I think the 'churn and burn' reputation is a fallacy. When I came here, I thought I would do my couple of years, get it on my résumé, and go work somewhere else. I have to say, in thirty-one years, I've never thought of leaving. If that sentiment is out there, it's because people know that we are very intense. We work hard, but we play hard too. Importantly, we go to great lengths to support our people throughout their careers."

Accenture's innovative work/life balance programs often support the "play hard" side of that equation. Their Live Well program encourages health and wellness, sometimes with a competitive spirit. For example, the Biggest Winner challenge was a twelve-week contest where employees set specific goals, track their progress, and win recognition and prizes from their teammates. Accenture offers new challenges during the year, with recent examples being a four-week Maintain Don't Gain challenge during the winter holidays and an eight-week Summer Shape Up challenge. One Accenture employee mused, "With the Biggest Winner, we had a team competition going between a few of us so I challenged myself to keep pace with my coworker across the aisle. Because of the challenge, I have lost over eighty pounds, reduced my cholesterol and blood sugars, and gotten my blood pressure under control. . . . It's really been a life changer."

Accenture also offers generous vacation time, and Take Five Days allows employees to take an additional five unpaid days off if they exhaust their allotted paid time off. As mentioned in Chapter 1, Future Leave is also an example of Accenture's efforts to ensure a sense of work/life balance. Essentially a self-funded sabbatical, employees may "bank" salary in order to take up to three months away from work with continued benefits, and they are assisted in the transition to and from their sabbatical.

Project teams also are encouraged to be creative in helping employees to meet the demands of the client as well as their "home team." In the Home Team Advantage program, managers keep a calendar of employees' family events so the team can anticipate and support employee absences. Employees are also encouraged to adopt the 3–4–5 model: spend three nights and four days out of town each week (a major aspect of a consultant's job has historically involved travel that did not allow for full weekends at home), and use the fifth day to work from anywhere. But Accenture hasn't stopped there. Their new Smart Work initiative aims to bring even more work/life balance by using new technology tools that will further reduce the need for travel, and the Local Market Initiative focuses on staffing clients with local Accenture teams to further reduce travel. It is this creativity and refusal to surrender that makes Accenture a great place to work.

Consulting firms aren't the only place you'll find employees under pressure to meet client demands. Liz Price, Attorney Hiring Partner at Atlanta-based law firm Alston & Bird, also talked about unique ways the firm handles the ongoing pressure for client-facing work. While most attorneys are likely to bill 2,000 hours per year, they often need to work one and a half to two hours for each hour that can be billed, meaning that sixty- to eighty-hour workweeks are not uncommon. But the only number that is considered for promotion to partner at most firms is the number of hours billed. Price told us, "At Alston & Bird, if you compared the total number of hours our lawyers work to the top hundred law firms, the total number of hours might be similar, but the quality would be much different. We track what we call 'non-billable hours.' We'll tell people who come over from other firms that they have to track their non-billable hours. You need to record that time because that tells us you're invested in this place and our future together." Attorneys are also encouraged to do one hundred hours of pro bono work each year, which also counts toward total hours billed while allowing them to give back to the community in ways they feel passionately about.

The additional issue that faces most law firms, however, is the status differential that can disrupt employees' sense of fairness and camaraderie. Traditionally, law firms have treated partners and attorneys with one set of standards, while support staff members receive the lesser end of the deal. Not so at Alston & Bird. One staff person told us, "I've been here twelve years and I can think of one specific time where I was disrespected by a partner. I can think of at least 999 times where I was treated with complete respect by a partner. I'll take that percentage any day of the week. My employees responsible for facilitating training sessions say the same thing to me. They're always amazed, especially when we have partners mixed in classes with secretaries, they learn together and respect each other."

Additionally, Liz Price says, "People understand that we're very much an egalitarian group. There's not a lot of hierarchy. One thing I'll always recommend to people looking to see if we are the right firm to join is to look at people's nameplates. A lot of times at other firms, the attorneys will be 'Mr. Hays' or 'Ms. Price.' The non-lawyers will be 'Jane Smith.' Here, it's 'Liz Price' and 'Jane Smith.' You're not a big deal just because you're a lawyer. In fact, there are many people here who will know a lot more than you do when you first start. You need to go to them and treat them with respect because they can help you a whole lot or not much at all."

The seeds of this egalitarian approach are planted even before the attorney joins the firm. On their "careers" website, Alston & Bird includes "Tips for Law Students," one of them being, "Alston & Bird has a very inclusive culture. Every interaction you have with an individual—not just the lawyers—at the firm matters." Here, unlike at other professional services firms, status isn't the secret currency that buys you a great workplace experience. Rather, everyone is expected to contribute to an inclusive culture, and potential hires are encouraged to think twice about joining the firm if they don't believe they can contribute in a meaningful way.

While professional services deal with the constant pressure of client demands and the status differentials inherent in firms with a clear career path and hierarchy, they do enjoy flexibility with regard to when and where their people work, which is not the case everywhere. The manufacturing industry is where we hear the most about the lack of flexibility as an obstacle to a great workplace, and we turn to it next.

Manufacturing: Clear Line of Sight and Flexibility

The two challenges that manufacturing managers share with us most often are the nature of the work itself and the lack of flexibility in accomplishing it. Unionization is sometimes suggested as a concern as well, but we'll address that challenge (which is not *external* but rather derives from the nature of the employees) in Chapter 8.

With regard to the nature of the work itself, there is obviously a range of manufacturing processes, from customized assembly to mass production. While all types of manufacturing environments have challenges, managers in mass production environments are often doubly tested. In these environments, employees typically find themselves performing a very specific process that may or may not readily connect to the mission and vision of the organization. At its extreme, the work is taxing, done in a loud and sometimes dangerous environment, and pressures to obtain short-term results in either production or error-reduction are great.

When the scope of the job is narrow, it is challenging to create a sense of contribution to the goals of the organization. For instance, at W. L. Gore & Associates, their machine operators' central tasks involve: "entering the parameters for machine production, loading the machine with relevant materials (i.e., glue, ink, etc. and including laminate rolls), maintaining the machine accordingly to standard procedures and starting/stopping the process whenever necessary." When employees do this work day to day, it takes extra effort to make the connection to a larger purpose, which is "to make money and have fun doing so" according to founder Bill Gore.

The first step in addressing this challenge is to remember that a sense of contribution is at the heart of employee pride, a hallmark of great workplaces. Just as importantly, knowing how your work impacts the lives of others—no matter how indirectly—can bring a sense of purpose to the work that transcends the immediate product or outcome. That's why managers in best companies, manufacturing and otherwise, take an opportunity to connect to a higher purpose at every turn for employees who hold jobs with a narrow scope. Communications reference the impact of employees' work. Reward systems are built to connect outcomes to mission fulfillment and the upholding of organizational values. And every employee gets the message that they matter, no matter how inconsequential their job may seem.

Taking the time to connect with employees doesn't have to involve complex or particularly innovative practices. For instance, organizations like Colgate Palmolive, a consumer products manufacturer, and Monsanto, an agriculture products producer, hold town hall meetings for their manufacturing employees. Everyone is invited, and the meetings offer the opportunity for face-to-face conversation with leaders. At W. L. Gore & Associates, one employee is named a "water carrier" every other month, an honor received for taking actions that perpetuate the unique Gore culture.

Making personal connections is also important. David Klassen, Devon Energy's Director of Corporate Communications, told us about the need for connecting with smaller groups. "We have a program called Coffee Talks. Once a month, we randomly select twenty employees and invite them to a breakfast. They sit down with one of our executive committee members. There's no agenda or script, just an informal discussion of whatever the employees want to talk about. The response we've gotten from our employees is off the charts. They love it."

But, even informal events aren't needed to create and perpetuate a sense of purpose. Rather, signaling that all employees matter in reaching a higher purpose can be as simple as the language managers use. Dr. John Noseworthy, President and CEO of Mayo Clinic, told us, "Our staff have asked me, 'Who's more important—the patients or us?' I say, 'The patients, by a hair, because the needs of the patients come first.' We will do everything under creation to develop our staff, but the purpose of having a staff is to meet the needs of our patients. When we speak

113

to our staff, we remind them that they are our most precious resource."

Despite the narrowness of some manufacturing roles, leaders in great workplaces manage to create a meaningful experience for their employees through rewards, communication, and the subtleties of language.

The other aspect of manufacturing environments that often shows up as an "excuse" is the lack of flexibility. While limited flextime may be possible in some organizations, working from home is often out of the question. Moreover, standards in both production and safety limit the degree of autonomy employees enjoy.

We sympathize with production managers when it comes to flexibility, and we often find that we don't have much in the way of directive advice when it comes to how to make production environments more flexible. But similar to our comments about work/life balance, the best companies keep trying to find a way, and that matters to employees. Balfour Beatty, a global construction and engineering services firm, experiments to find programs that fit the needs of the business and their employees, putting pilot programs into place wherever it makes sense. Their efforts at finding work/life balance have included early release Fridays, rotating Fridays off, and company-paid health club memberships.

With regard to safety, managers in best companies shift the conversation from the standards themselves to the reason for adhering to them. In other words, they use the safety standards as an inroad to conversations about respect, caring, and teamwork rather than focusing on compliance and consequences.

In some companies, this focus on safety can indirectly increase candid communication and feedback. At aluminum producer Alcoa, CEO Paul O'Neil famously shifted the culture to one of initiative-taking and excellence through his focus on safety. In a

2001 article on Alcoa's turnaround, Merrill Lynch analyst Daniel A. Roling said, "What stands out is [O'Neil's] absolute commitment to delegating responsibility."[2] The delegation requirements of a safe environment spilled over into other aspects of the business. Stories of O'Neil's success abound, but all of them suggest that while safety is the focal point, the fact that he made everyone responsible for it necessitated greater communication, collaboration, and a shared responsibility for success that went beyond safe behaviors and incited a culture dedicated to excellence in all aspects of Alcoa's performance.

Dr. Noseworthy at Mayo Clinic also described how the behaviors required for a safe environment go beyond directives and OSHA standards. Rather, they are by-products of collaboration and hallmarks of the Mayo culture. "Safety includes when is it safe for a nurse to tell the surgeon that she thinks the surgeon is about to make a mistake. The culture of safety is a strong commitment of the organization. We have disciplined, intentional processes that we invest in heavily to further educate our staff, encouraging humility, encouraging development, encouraging listening and never tolerating behavior that makes people fearful or is disrespectful."

While the challenges in manufacturing are in creating a clear line of sight and purpose despite strict standards of performance, the responses in great workplaces are to continue to challenge the industry norms on flexibility, and to use safety to signal caring and concern.

Not-for-Profit: Doing More with Less

While the need to do more with less is a perennial challenge in the not-for-profit world, many companies have dealt with this in the aftermath of the mid-2000s economic downturn. Yet, they are still great places to work. Again, it doesn't take a huge budget or a fancy title to demonstrate credibility, respect, and fairness. If you can build a relationship, you can create a great workplace. You can strengthen ties with employees regardless of your access to money or your ability to set HR policy for perks and benefits.

While large budgets are nice, especially when it comes to creating a great workplace experience, they can also mask the need for employees to cooperate, collaborate, and innovate in service of the organization's mission and vision. When cash is plentiful, it's easy to throw resources at a problem and gloss over the employee interdependencies that can be leveraged in service of a solution. If my department needs to make an emergency shipment to an important client, I might hire contractors to get the work done when in times of financial liquidity. However, when resources are tight, I am forced to work with my peers to reallocate resources and reprioritize collective goals. This creates a better understanding of the organization's direction, better relationships with my coworkers, and a pride in accomplishment that is so much stronger than that which could come from writing a check.

Perhaps tighter budgets are why not-for-profit organizations are a bit better at addressing the challenge of resource shortages; people come in to the organization assuming they won't have cash to throw around. And just as the obstacle of safety opens up avenues for communication in manufacturing jobs, reduced budgets come with increased dedication and cooperation—but only if it is seen as an operating *condition* rather than a *constraint.* Not-for-profit organizations have a natural opportunity to inspire employees to band together to overcome resource shortages. One manager at Teach for America told us, "I think we probably all have [a 'no excuses'] approach to our work. If we need something, we'll find a way to figure it out."

116

This "can do" attitude is certainly an outcome of the disciplined hiring at Teach for America, but it also pays off in the ways employees contribute to the mission that are not formalized in a job description. For instance, one Teach for America associate responsible for facilities maintenance, Chris, is said to "race around each day serving the needs of over 400 staff people by restocking their supplies and fixing broken desks and printers all while planning how best to raise more funds for the mission he is so deeply invested in. Chris has leveraged personal connections to find his way in front of several small philanthropist boards and persuaded them to support Teach for America by making considerable donations on an annual basis. Though it's nowhere within his job description, he has raised over $10,000 for the organization." While Chris was inspired to address the resource challenges by initiating a fundraising drive, other employees (especially in for-profit companies) find ways to cut costs or reallocate time in order to do so.

Like in not-for-profits, the best for-profit companies emerged from the financial downturn with a stronger sense of resourcefulness, and perhaps stronger commitments from their employees. Whether being deliberate about which costs are to be cut, using downtime wisely, or explicitly communicating about the future, a message is sent to (or reinforced with) employees about their importance to the organization. At Men's Wearhouse, leaders made the decision to cut travel, but maintain events that build camaraderie. At Accenture, reduced client work translated to employee betterment. Jill Smart put it this way: "[W]e thought we could use the time to give our people more training so that when we come out of this, they're more engaged and more deeply trained."

Lest they leave the messaging to chance, leaders and managers in great workplaces increase communication during times of economic uncertainty. In 2008, after undergoing an 8 percent reduction in force at the request of their investors, Zappos CEO Tony Hsieh wrote the following on his blog: "I know that many tears were shed today, both by laid-off and non-laid-off employees alike. Given our family culture, our layoffs are much tougher emotionally than they would be at many other companies. . . . These are tough times for everyone, and I'm sure there will be many follow up questions to this email. If you have any questions about your specific job or department, please talk to your department manager. For all other questions, comments, or thoughts, please feel free to email me." Employees feel the effects of a reduced bottom line, whether it be from reduced profits or reduced expenditures. Addressing the situation directly helps employees know that their leaders both understand and are working to reverse the negative impact.

When it comes to resource shortages, be they a function of the organization's legal entity (like not-for-profits) or short-term deficiencies, managers need to attend to *how* those challenges are addressed as much, if not more, than *what* is done to address them. It is important to rally the troops around a common goal, encourage and model collaboration, and communicate openly and honestly.

Other macro forces are often at the heart of manager challenges to creating a great workplace, but they are so macro that they transcend the boundaries of industry we've discussed so far. One is social in nature (controversy), and the other is geographic dispersion, which impacts workplaces whether dispersed within the U.S. or globally.

THE "HUNKER DOWN" EXCUSE

Sometimes managers don't believe that their workplace can be a great one because of its controversial products or negative press.

One manager we worked with, Jim Vickberg, told us that it is hard to inspire a sense of purpose and pride when the news highlights the company's shortcomings. Conversations about the greater good devolve quickly, and it becomes clear that employees continue to work at the organization only because they feel they have no other choice.

While this may be Jim's presenting challenge, our experience is that controversy really isn't the problem. The lack of an organizational identity and sense of purpose speaks louder to employees than any external controversial message. We covered organizational identity in Chapter 3, and heeding the advice in that chapter may deflect most of the challenges that come from negative press or social sentiment. But, speaking directly to Jim, and other managers who feel that the controversy itself is insurmountable, we offer the following.

Great Place to Work® Institute has always taken the stance that great workplaces are great because of the experience of their employees. According to Robert Levering, co-founder of the Institute, "Our position is that we, as evaluators, are evaluating the quality of the workplace from the viewpoint of its employees. We do *not* judge companies on the basis of their products, services, business practices, CSR activities, quality processes, or financial performance. We leave it to others to judge companies from the viewpoint of the customer, the community, or the investor." While this line in the sand is helpful when evaluating hundreds of companies each year for list membership, it does not speak to the boots-on-the-ground challenges that managers may have when their industry is under fire.

The data are there, however, to back up Levering's point; we find employees in great workplaces are proud of their organizations despite a level of negative social sentiment. So if an organization's industry is under scrutiny, what *does* that mean for employees in its workplaces? What does it mean to create a sense of identity that can withstand scrutiny about the industry to which the organization belongs?

Monsanto, a Great Place to Work® Institute list-making company in Latin America, India, and the U.S., is a company that has seen more than its share of negative press about its promotion of genetically modified foods and their impact upon family farms. About Monsanto, Levering said, "We took a careful look at Monsanto's employee comments, as that gives us the most data about how the employees feel about the company. We were especially curious whether any of them were disturbed about the impact of the products they make. On the contrary, there were numerous comments from employees praising their products. Many of them stated strongly that they felt that Monsanto was making a better world as a result of their genetically modified and other such products."

In order to create such a strong sense of pride, Monsanto must create and sustain an organizational identity that has a stronger pull than the constant barrage of press. Bedrock to that identity is the Monsanto Pledge, a declaration of values, which unifies employees through its prominence in all of Monsanto's employee efforts. One project manager said: "The Monsanto Pledge has been a very powerful element of shaping our culture. It helps us reach decisions about the work we do and provides inspiration to help us find new solutions to provide for the world's growing population." Monsanto also rewards people for living the values outlined in the pledge while creating value for the company. Last but not least, Monsanto is adamant about ensuring their impact on the environment and human rights is as low as it can possibly be. While people on the outside may disagree with their mission, goals, and approach, Monsanto's virtuous attention to global concerns and its clear direction for employees make it a great workplace.

The oil and gas industry has also come under fire in recent years for its perceived contribution to environmental degradation and the way its wealth seems impervious to economic forces. David Eberhardt, Devon Energy's Director of HR Strategy and Systems, says that their industry is often misunderstood, and that employees see it very differently than the public does. "I think our industry gets demonized. It's not demonized internally. All of our people are proud of our industry and what we do. I think what also might be misunderstood in the political conversation is how committed our people are to preserving the environment. Many geologists get into geology because they love being outside and exploring the earth. They're not out there trying to figure out ways to destroy it. They are trying to make a living, but at the same time, they're cognizant of the effects of drilling and they're very committed to doing that in a way that limits our impact on the environment. There is a strong sense of pride and commitment to keeping the earth clean."

Again, Devon goes to great lengths to create a strong sense of identity. One of their values is "Be a Good Neighbor," which is further described this way: "With the continued expansion of our business, the spectrum of communities that are touched by our operations continually broadens. That is why we have a fundamental respect for the environment and the people and communities in which we operate." Stories told by their managers show the way the company has acted on this value. For reasons not clear at the time, a portion of Lake Weatherford in Texas became discolored one day in 2009. Local officials called Devon, suspecting that one of their nearby drilling sites might be the cause. Two operations supervisors from a nearby plant arrived quickly to help assess the situation. Even after it was determined that the Devon well wasn't the cause, Devon employees stayed on site to clean the discoloration and collect soil and water samples.

This example shows their dedication to the communities in which they operate, and their commitment to the natural environment near their operations.

Despite the social forces acting against employees' sense of pride and contribution in these and other industries, their managers create and reinforce a sense of identity that inspires employees and contributes to their sense of trust, pride, and camaraderie. A strong sense of identity can also help with a different challenge that impacts companies across industries: size and global reach.

THE "TOO BIG" EXCUSE

We are constantly reminded that we live in a global world. There were more than 3,000 multinational corporations in the U.S. alone in 2008. What's more, companies are getting larger; nearly 2,000 U.S. organizations have more than 5,000 employees.[3] As the size of the workforce, the number of locations, and the global presence of organizations increase, so too do the challenges for managers creating great workplaces. Two questions often come up about how to manage size and geographic dispersion: How do you create a sense of identity across multiple locations? And how do you create person-to-person connectedness?

A sense of identity is challenging in one location with a few hundred employees, let alone several hundreds of locations, a few thousand employees, and the added pressure of distinct cultures, languages, and time zones. Even leaders at the best companies are tested by the trend toward true globalization, where managers may live half a world away from their teams. Jill Smart of Accenture told us, "My head of HR Strategy lives in Singapore. My new Chief Learning Officer is from India but currently living in Singapore. It's really a struggle to find hours of the day that are convenient for all of us. From a day-to-day perspective, that's the biggest challenge. I would say that maintaining the culture when you're big takes more work. It has to be more proactive. It takes more work to have the glue that keeps the pieces together."

On the World's Best Multinationals list, produced by Great Place to Work® Institute, the number of employees ranges from 6,700 at National Instruments to 1,850,000 employed by McDonald's. Though it's challenging, these organizations create a sense of identity much like a smaller company would—through a common set of values that are reinforced through orientation, communication, and rewards.

Marriott, with 350,000 at headquarters, managed and franchised properties worldwide, ensures that managers know, teach, and role model the company's five core values. As part of the "Living Our Core Values" program, which is refreshed annually, general managers at all managed hotels take time to conduct small group sessions with their associates, discussing issues important to them, such as saving for retirement, or even how to open a checking account or get a car loan. Ultimately, the practice ensures the commitment and active participation of everyone in the company—from top to bottom—in making Marriott a great workplace.

While the way the values are discussed and upheld may differ from location to location, managers find the common threads and provide a sense of cohesiveness to the employee experience. Even when a consistent identity is possible across multiple locations, though, a sense of team is harder to create. After all, you may not ever meet the majority of your colleagues in the organization. Some companies, such as W. L. Gore & Associates, have dealt with this very directly, by keeping its plants and locations small enough that people feel a strong sense of community. (It turns out that Gore's magic number is less than 200 employees in a single location.)

Other companies have created more virtual ways for employees to feel connected to one another, even if they rarely get the chance to interact personally. Zappos employees play the Zappos Family Face Game. Their intranet site is a part of every employee's daily experience. When employees log on, they play a quick round of the Face Game. A randomly selected employee's picture pops up and employees are asked to guess the employee's name. Regardless if the response is right or wrong, the pictured employee's name and personal bio comes up, and the employees logging on are asked if they know him or her. Zappos tracks these relationships to see how far-reaching employees' interactions are. This way they can develop ways to assist employees in forming relationships outside their direct daily team-based interactions.

Teach for America also helps employees collaborate across multiple locations. One manager told us, "I head up the facilities team and we have over fifty-five offices across the country. We've created a community of office managers and a professional learning community where we all get together regularly on the telephone and collaborate. We talk about culture an enormous amount. How can we bring that culture to each of our offices? How can we share our resources, which is absolutely critical for a non-profit organization? How can we use each other's ideas? I say that you can have a great idea in your own office and you can be super impactful, or you can share your idea with fifty-five offices and be impactful beyond belief. I think we've done a really good job of creating that community of collaborators and finding better ways to execute."

As technologically savvy as these companies are, most would agree there is no substitute for a face-to-face meeting. The Coca-Cola Company embraces its global reach, and aims to share processes and tools rather than reinvent them every time they enter a new market or region. One way they do this is pulling together people within a particular business unit who are located all over the world. One manager told us: "At a global meeting, I sit with the other brand managers from around the world, and we have such commonalities between what we were trying to do. There were many more commonalities than differences. That sense of global community is very powerful. Getting to know friends from all over the world is part of what makes Coca-Cola a great workplace."

Creating a sense of identity, community, and collaboration is more difficult once the size and reach of the organization increases, but it also comes with its advantages. The number of perspectives increases, the number of experiences increases, and ultimately no employee should ever feel as though he or she is solving problems alone. But, managers need to do their part by making sure everyone is pulling in the same direction, and that they work together as they do.

WHAT TO DO NEXT

Several forces impact your organization, be they social, economic, or a by-product of your industry. Though the effects of such systemic forces may seem insurmountable, they aren't. It just takes a bit more effort for you than it may for others outside of your industry or organization. Immediately, you can

- See every decision, even those that need to be made to ensure the mere survival of the organization, as human decisions. Take care to build relationships when making the decision, and beyond.
- Reverse any assumptions you have about the uniqueness of your industry. "We are so different," becomes "we have challenges just like everyone else."

125

○ Be honest about the demands of your workplace, and hire people who are energized by them.

○ Reframe what you think about workplace flexibility in terms of what you *can* do rather than what you *can't*.

○ When you can't do much to make the workplace more flexible, put support mechanisms in place to help the demands of the work environment feel a bit more feasible.

○ Create a clear line of sight from even the most mundane jobs to the ultimate value creation of the organization.

○ Don't underestimate the importance of showing up, whether to answer questions for employees on the shop floor or visiting your team located hundreds of miles away.

○ Use compliance requirements and resource shortages to achieve collaboration and shared responsibility at all levels of the organization.

○ Revisit your organization's identity and be sure your practices and day-to-day interactions reinforce its meaning for employees.

CHAPTER 7

IT'S JUST NOT THE RIGHT TIME

Managers we speak with will often share with us that "now is just not the right time" to focus on this issue because we are "undergoing a leadership change at the top" or "just started merging with another business," or our favorite, "we just had a layoff." Now, they insist, is definitely not the right time to begin such an effort. From their point of view, the nature of the event seems at odds with a counter-effort to create a great workplace. One manager shared with us that a recent plant closing is going to "negatively impact any trust-building efforts, so shouldn't we let the dust settle first?" The answer, of course, is no. If a plant closing (or any of the events we discuss in this chapter) might negatively impact the workplace, wouldn't it make sense to have a counter-strategy to mitigate those effects and build trust?

You have likely heard the saying "The only thing constant is change." The nature of business is that business is always changing. Everyone seems to be talking about being more "agile," implying that managers need to be flexible, nimble, and quick when it comes to product development, to customer service, to market demands, to sales processes, to—well, to everything. Organizations need to be responsive to megatrends such as globalization and the rise of emerging markets, technological innovations, regional conflicts and civil unrest, and global energy consumption in the face of a warming planet. These and other megatrends shape how organizations of all sizes, locations, and industries think about their business strategy. But events that arise from these trends should not serve as an excuse.

In this changing landscape, an organization's growth is often charted by the very presence of new or disruptive events, activities, programs, and tactics that change the way we approach our work. The more change there is, the more the organization must be growing. When a disruptive event occurs, it upsets the natural flow of work and work relationships. When a manager's team doubles in size because the organization went through a merger, questions about who these new team members are, how we will all work together, and how our goals will change naturally arise. People need time to integrate the change into their work habits and align to the "new normal." Our experience tells us when we take the time and energy to create high-trust relationships, that work actually supports quicker adoption of the change efforts and how the manager and his team will manage the event. Far from being a "bad" time to consider your great workplace efforts, disruptive events or innovations might be the "best" time to engage in such efforts!

By our measure, a cognitive obstacle may also be at play here. The most likely obstacle, as we discussed in Chapter 2, is the thinking that great workplaces were born that way. Perhaps you think that great workplaces already have it "all together," and they don't have to work very hard to keep up a high-trust culture. Or perhaps you think that disruptive events don't happen at great workplaces. They do. Organizations with great workplace cultures aren't immune to the larger economic and social trends and issues that we all have to face. But invariably these organizations have chosen a posture or attitude that not only welcomes change but *seeks out* changes. When we sat down with Gwen McDonald, the Chief HR Officer at NetApp, she shared that it's important for the stability of the workplace culture to not be at the expense of any changes that are taking place. "We talk about change as constant," she said. "What does change really mean? On some level, that means some negotiation of power. That's a challenge and an opportunity. When we're looking at change, it's easy to say that it'll impact our culture. Sometimes culture is used as an excuse for not wanting to change. We need to ensure that culture is not the bad guy."

In this chapter, we will consider various types of disruptive events: mergers and acquisitions; changes in leadership; layoffs; internal changes and spikes; and external events like terrorism and other societal changes. We'll provide examples of how disruptive events tend to play out in organizations, and how best companies approach them. We'll also offer some recommendations and best practices for how you can use disruptive events (both unforeseen and known) as opportunities to building a high-trust workplace.

DISRUPTIVE EVENTS COME IN ALL SHAPES AND SIZES

Sometimes disruptive events are of a company's own making, such as a merger with another entity, while at other times external events demand a response from a company, such as when there is some sort of social unrest. Sometimes the event is like an earthquake in that it is short in duration but powerful, and at other times the event is experienced over a much longer period of time and the effects are cumulative. Disruptive events tend to share three common characteristics. First, the impact of the event fundamentally changes business processes. Second, the emergence of the event results in a sense of disorientation, loss, confusion

129

with employees and other stakeholders. And third, it takes the company time to reach a new equilibrium.

Mergers and Acquisitions

Mergers and acquisitions (or their cousin, divestitures) are a common occurrence in businesses today. Professional services firm Bain & Company note that the numbers of mergers and acquisitions (M&A) taking place tend to be cyclical, and that we will likely see a renaissance in M&A as a core business strategy.[1] Indeed, there is a long history of M&As stretching back to the late 1800s, and they have tended to occur in waves. More recently, the Institute for Mergers, Acquisitions, and Alliances notes that in 2012 alone, close to 40,000 separate merger and acquisition transactions occurred globally worth an estimated $4 trillion (USD); M&As are a function of many businesses' growth strategy, and it is big business

However, Clayton Christensen and his colleagues note that study after study puts the failure rate of M&As between 70 and 90 percent.[2] This is an incredibly high failure rate for a business strategy that requires significant resources and planning to execute. Even if we optimistically put the failure rate of M&As around 50 percent, as Robert Sher suggests,[3] that still is a high risk growth strategy. With so much risk, why would businesses bank on these types of disruptive events? Because the potential payoff is tremendous. And that is why these disruptive events are a common feature of global business life.

It is important to note, however, that one of the major reasons why M&As fail to meet their financial targets are the challenges in combining organizational cultures.[4] We'll explore this a little more in this chapter, but it's worthwhile pointing out here that *not* focusing on creating a great workplace culture now can have a potential negative impact in the future.

Leadership Changes

Leadership changes by their very nature are disruptive events because new leaders tend to want to move the organization in new directions or change different aspects of the workplace culture. In fact, sometimes they are brought in for the sole purpose of doing so, such as Marissa Meyer's appointment to CEO of Yahoo! in 2012. The very announcement of a leadership change can result in a period of uncertainty and (sometimes) fear, followed by a new leader at the top of the organization, and then another period of uncertainty. It takes time for the organization to understand the intent and new direction of the leader, and then align itself to where the leader wishes to take the organization (if the leader has the credibility and competence to do so).

In a May 2012 study, Booz & Company noted that the CEO turnover at the world's largest 2,500 public companies returned to rates seen during the pre-recession years, and that 14.2 percent of CEOs at the world's largest companies were replaced.[5] In some countries, such as Japan, the CEO turnover rate was around 19 percent—almost 1 out of 5 businesses saw a change at the top. Every time an organization welcomes a new chief executive, there is a subsequent change for the organization. The change is usually one of direction or strategy, but sometimes culture too. Culture is more challenging to change, but we have seen new leaders recast the organization's identity in powerful ways, resulting in a new workplace culture. For example, one healthcare organization we worked with had a change of CEOs. The new CEO implemented a new program of values, business strategy, rewards

131

systems, and management structure in order to create a more "safety first" culture.

Layoffs

Layoffs are a particularly wrenching disruptive event for an organization. While the employees that are let go experience the biggest impact, all employees (and even other stakeholders such as customers) are also impacted by a layoff. As in other types of disruptive events, the loss of employees results in new ways in which business is conducted and new business processes develop. A layoff results in a sense of loss and confusion at what this might mean for the organization, and perhaps anger and fear at colleagues being let go or that such an event might happen again.

In 2011, employers initiated 6,597 extended mass layoff events that resulted in the separation of more than 1.1 million workers in the U.S. according to recent BLS statistics.[6] The "great recession" of 2008 impacted workers around the world, of course, and not just in the United States. As of the time of this book, the global economy continues to be sluggish, with several countries sustaining high unemployment or underemployment. In Spain, for example, youth unemployment is 55 percent. Business today has many euphemisms for layoffs, including *downsizing, rightsizing, delayering,* etc. Whatever it is called, however, it is still about people losing their jobs.

Internal Changes and Spikes

Regular internal business issues sometimes become disruptive events, things like the adoption of technology (anyone who has ever lived through a technological system integration knows what we are talking about), succession planning, or the happy problem of having to hire a lot of workers because of a spike in demand. These issues are disruptive events because they have a significant impact on business processes, resources, or goals. And they are often accompanied by an impact on productivity and culture as well.

Terrorism and Societal Unrest

While we won't discuss societal unrest too much in this chapter, it is important to note that these events are also disruptive to organizational life. External social, environmental, and political events can also have an unsettling impact on your ability to create a great work environment. They are a part of the larger picture of disruptive events that you might experience and have to manage through. Managers tend to see these as particular obstacles because the event is external to the organization, and often seen as not within their control.

As an example, take the September 11th terrorist attack on the United States that caused global markets to drop sharply. It was only the third time in the New York Stock Exchange's history that it had a prolonged closure. The attack resulted in $40 billion in insurance losses alone.[7] This doesn't include the impact on aviation, tourism, the stock and bond markets, and other industries and businesses. This disruptive event had and continues to have a major impact on the global economy and how businesses operate. Think for a second about the differences you experience in traveling pre- versus post-9/11. Entire organizations, processes, and systems have been set up or restructured as a result of that event, and it impacts how we develop and engage in business.

Take a different external societal event—the Arab Spring of 2011. In a January 2012 post on Knowledge@Wharton blog, they note that "the obvious economic victims of the Arab Spring have

133

been the countries that witnessed the most violent protests. Egypt's economy, for instance, has suffered steep hits to its vital tourism segment. Representing 10 percent of the country's GDP, Egypt's tourism revenues are at $9 billion for 2011, down one-third from the previous year."[8] On a global scale, the biggest negative impact on business has been in North America, where a quarter of businesses report having sustained a negative impact due to the global supply chain for oil and other goods. This is remarkable, considering that the unrest was half a world away. Organizations everywhere are impacted by having to respond to this type of event, making leaders' responses to change an important feature of workplace culture.

Last but not least, many companies have had to deal with events (often of their own making) wherein there was a displeased or angry response on the part of consumers, investors, or the larger public. The public outcry after Enron imploded may be one of the most well-known cases. But product recalls like the one Toyota had a couple of years ago can also create unforeseen challenges in managing the business, let alone creating a great workplace.

All of these various issues that we have raised so far are examples of disruptive events. Rather than being obstacles to creating a great workplace, they can be the reason to create a great workplace! In the remainder of the chapter, we will discuss what makes these events so disruptive to begin with and how we see best companies deal with such events *while* sustaining a high level of trust.

WHAT MAKES DISRUPTIVE EVENTS DISRUPTIVE?

Carol is a product manager at a pharmaceutical company. She has been with the company for close to fifteen years, and has held several different jobs in that time. "I came because the firm was big enough that I could do a lot of different things," she told us. "The pharmaceutical industry has always been exciting to me. . . . It is always changing." Recently, her firm acquired another firm of roughly the same size. Carol explained, "This has been really difficult because [the other firm] has a great product pipeline that is a good complement to us in that respect, but they have a completely different set of values and bringing the two employee groups together has not been easy."

For instance, Carol shared that communication is not as efficient and easy as it once was. New norms of when to communicate, how much to communicate, who needs to be involved, and so on needed to be figured out. "Employees from [the other firm] cc everyone, and so my email tripled. It's little things like that, but also a lot of big things." Big things for Carol included basic work flow processes, how resources are allocated, and how decisions are made. Trying to work through all of that has taken time, energy, and concentration. For Carol, supporting her team through this transition has been a key consideration.

When we spoke with members of her team, they shared with us that Carol has tried to reduce the ambiguity and confusion, the fatigue and stress that comes with change, and create a sense of "safety." She has encouraged people to raise questions and concerns. "There is a lot that is unknown, but Carol helps keep us focused on the here and now," explained one of her staff. "Not knowing has been the biggest stress."

In 1946, scientist Hans Selye examined the effects of stress on the body, and came up with what's called General Adaption Syndrome—which is exactly what Carol is trying to protect her people against. The first stage is Alarm. You recognize that there is danger and prepare to deal with it (a.k.a. the fight-or-flight response). Next, the body shifts to Resistance. The sources of stress are possibly resolved in this stage. While your stress

135

hormones may have returned to normal levels, you may have reduced defenses and adaptive energy left. If the threat or change isn't resolved, and you continued to feel stressed, then you will enter the third phase. The third phase is the Exhaustion stage, and here your body's ability to resist is lost because its adaption energy is sapped.[9] We often refer to this stage as *burnout*, because the stress level is up and stays up. Any of the disruptive events discussed at the start of the chapter can result in employees (and managers) undergoing this syndrome. Helping employees through the stress response is one way to frame the manager's role during this time.

Disruptive events are disruptive precisely because they change the nature of the work environment, and potentially the psychological contract (that unspoken understanding of what is expected and gained in the employment relationship) that employees and their employers have developed. These events typically don't have a clear road map, and it takes time to figure out what the right path is. While employees and their managers are experiencing the fuzzy front end of the change process, uncertainty and ambiguity represent real obstacles to the trust relationships that are needed at just such a moment. In this light, a different model, Affective Events Theory, is a useful construct for us as it helps explain how what we feel about a particular event informs how we think about our work and our commitment.

Affective Events Theory (AET) is a model developed by organizational psychologists Weiss and Cropanzano that explains how emotions and moods influence job performance and job satisfaction.[10] It explains the links between an employee's mental or emotional state and their reaction to an incident that affects their commitment, performance, and satisfaction. AET proposes that certain work behaviors are best explained by an employee's emotions or mood. It also suggests that cognitive behaviors are the best predictors of job satisfaction. Essentially, how we feel about an event or incident (such as an acquisition by another company) determines how we think and evaluate our level of commitment to the organization and our job satisfaction.

Similarly, Kusstatscher and Cooper suggest that job satisfaction, mental attitude, and one's emotions can be seen as related constructs.[11] Job satisfaction tends to have an emotional component or cause. They cite research about job satisfaction in the M&A context and found that the level of job satisfaction with a merger was very strongly associated with several key variables, including one's satisfaction with supervision, satisfaction with career future and company identification, communication with top management, and agreement with the acquiring company's mission statement. In all of these ways, employee engagement has an underlying emotional component. And emotions give rise to thoughts that result in behaviors. It would make sense, then, to understand that disruptive events create powerful emotions that drive employee job satisfaction. In the example above, Carol was able to mitigate the impact of negative emotions by opening up a communication forum and creating a sense of safety, which dulls the intensity of the restlessness and agitation that come along with uncertainty.

EVENTS HAPPEN IN BEST COMPANIES TOO

Like you, managers at the best companies to work for also have to deal with disruptive events. These companies experience mergers and acquisitions, leadership changes, changes in direction or business model, and in the rare instance, layoffs. Managers at great workplaces are not immune from the forces of change and sometimes of circumstance, but they have taken a decidedly unique approach and used their company's identity and culture in service of creating a high-trust workplace.

137

Given the number of mergers and acquisitions that happen every year around the globe, it is no surprise that many of the best companies have gone through some sort of merger, have acquired other firms, or been themselves acquired. One thing we found with best companies is that they keep their firm's culture and values in plain sight. Said John Richels, the CEO of Devon Energy, "One of the big challenges, when you're growing a company through acquisition, is that you maintain a culture and you don't become rudderless in that area. We went to some real lengths over the last few years and I put a lot of personal effort into communicating who Devon is, what our culture is and what's important to us."

Since we can't address every possible type of disruptive event in this book, we've chosen to address the common themes we heard from managers about how they approach creating a high-trust culture in the midst of disruptive organizational events. First, we found that managers find their footing by determining which of their culture's strengths are not threatened by the event, and anchoring their efforts to those strengths. Second, they invest a lot of time in two-way dialogue with employees when disruptive events occur. Third, they think creatively and responsively regarding the challenge or underlying needs. Fourth, they focus on providing knowledge of the first step, so as to reassure employees that everything is okay, and reduce resistance to the event or change effort. And fifth, they ensure a basic sense of fairness and "we're all in this together." Together, these form a response template to building trust in the face of disruptive events.

Find Your Footing

Best companies tend to build upon their strengths. They understand their organizational identity very well, as we discussed in

138

Chapter 3. And managers use their firm's core strengths and culture as a way to respond to events that occur. "When Centex Construction was acquired by parent company Balfour Beatty, they continued their tradition of employee engagement and active investment in company culture," explained Connie Oliver, Vice President of Corporate Communications for the company. The newly named Balfour Beatty Construction was then recognized as a *FORTUNE* 100 best company four years in a row. As Oliver explained about their new parent company, "Balfour Beatty was truly one of those fantastic owners who said 'if it ain't broke, don't fix it.' They bought us because they liked what they saw, they liked the culture, they liked our processes and our leadership, and they said 'we aren't here to change you, but rather to benefit from what you do to support our global business.'" In comparing their new owner to their previous one, Oliver summarized, "We went from being the stepchild of a large homebuilding organization to becoming an active partner with a global engineering and infrastructure business. Balfour Beatty gets what we do and it's been a great partnership ever since." Time after time, we heard something very similar from managers at other best companies. A manager at The Coca-Cola Company remarked to us, "One of the biggest changes was when The Coca-Cola Company acquired the North American business of Coca-Cola Enterprises. There were two different cultures at Coca-Cola Enterprises and Coca-Cola North America. At the very beginning, I wondered how we were going to mesh them. The two organizations were very aware of and focused on that challenge. When we set out the 2020 Vision, senior leaders took what was important to the two organizations and brought them together, utilizing the best of both cultures."

At Zappos, this focus on building on the core was central in their acquisition by Amazon. The CFO, Chris Nielsen, shared with us: "The whole logic of the acquisition was built around the recognition that Zappos is a different place, we want it to be different going forward, we think it's important to retain that uniqueness, and collectively we don't want to mess that up. The first conversation [we had about the acquisition], we talked about a set of principles that we would use to define our relationship with Amazon. We wrote those down and we still refer to them. In those tenets, we also acknowledge that there are certain things we have to do as part of a public company. We'll keep those to a minimum, we'll be clear about what they are and we'll take care of them. An example of that is that we can't talk about our financials outside the normal time frames of earnings releases. Does that impinge on the core of who we are as a company? Frankly, it doesn't." Zappos created a context and a plan to help mitigate the natural upheaval that comes from an acquisition. They have been able to navigate through this change, keeping much of what is core and unique about them as a business.

When oil refiner Valero Energy of San Antonio merged with Ultramar Diamond Shamrock (UDS), Valero evaluated both companies' employee programs and selected the best ones for the newly combined organization. The improved set of benefits and resources included a Dialogue Dispute Resolution Program developed by Diamond Shamrock in 1994. This alternative means of settling disputes works at all levels and applies to any work-related conflict. Dialogue Advisors within the HR department are available to serve as neutral facilitators of the process, opening the lines of communication and developing solutions. The process has proven to be fair, simple, timely, and effective. In this way, Valero was able to build on the strengths of programs and practices that were already there, and extend the core.

As these managers from Balfour Beatty, Coca-Cola, and Zappos, and the example given of Valero suggest, it is important to start from where you are. When a disruptive event occurs, everything will seem out of kilter or somewhat discombobulated.

Start with what you know about your team, your department, or your organization. What is most useful about what you do and how you do it, and how can that be applied to the current circumstance? Starting with your strengths will help you find your footing, and accordingly make the change or disruptive event a little less scary. Your employees will appreciate your taking that extra step.

Create an Open Dialogue

We were going to label this section "Communicate!" but that seems too general to be helpful. Clearly, as a manager, you need to communicate with your people as much as you can, as soon as you can, when something happens. That will go a long way in enhancing credibility. Even if you have to be honest and say, "I don't know," that level of transparency and openness will increase your trustworthiness. But what we heard from managers was something a little different than just "communicate." They talked about needing to engage in an ongoing *dialogue* with employees—one that supported questioning, listening, reflection, and transparency.

For example, when one consumer goods company we've worked with decided to close three plant locations, they announced the closures twelve to eighteen months in advance (far above the sixty days required by law) to allow employees to adequately prepare for the transition. Many employees were offered positions/promotional opportunities at other locations, and those who were laid off were provided a financial transition package with job search assistance. But the company started by communicating information up front, and giving employees some time to deal with the news. As a result, employees were able to go through the "grief process" and receive support from the organization and their peers in the workplace. Employees were able to talk about their pain and confusion from the layoff, get to problem solving, and say good-bye when the time came to close the facilities.

When oil refiner Valero Energy merged with Ultramar Diamond Shamrock (UDS), Valero conducted a series of events to make UDS employees feel welcome in their new firm, including hosting a series of CEO meetings with intimate groups of employees at San Antonio headquarters of both firms to extend a welcome and answer questions. They held an open house at each headquarters, during which employees were greeted by top management and given guided tours of each campus, including the CEO's office, fitness center, and cafeteria. And there were numerous trips by the Valero CEO and senior management to all the former UDS facilities where they hosted barbecues and held roundtable meetings, among other communication activities. All of these activities were in service of creating a welcoming community from the beginning and ensuring that there was a high level of communication.

In our interviews, managers told us the importance of being present and available with employees, of listening and answering their questions in an honest, straightforward manner, and of sharing information openly and honestly. Creating an open dialogue will signal to employees that you understand that they may be anxious, and that you plan to help them as they maneuver through the disruptive event, whatever it is.

Think Creatively About How to Respond

Sometimes leaders know about disruptive events in advance. When an event such as a merger or a potential layoff is about to occur, it is useful to think about creative approaches to addressing real needs. It may take some time for you to brainstorm and think through how to address the event, but investing the time up front can be extraordinarily helpful. And sometimes, involving employees in the process can help them prepare for the event.

When it comes to layoffs, we suggest that organizations avoid them if at all possible. That may sound obvious, but trust us, it's not—many leaders jump to layoffs the moment the budget looks tight. Layoffs are among the most disruptive events a company can experience, and research suggests that they don't always meet the stated financial goals that helped drive the need for a layoff to begin with. So our first bit of advice is to think creatively about options other than a layoff. Look toward other options first, including hiring or pay freezes, voluntary severance or early retirement, or temporary part-time scheduling. Perhaps you redeploy people elsewhere in the company. The important point here is to put the idea of a layoff as the very last resort and consider other options first.

Thinking creatively about how to address the need to save money and minimize layoffs can result in some innovative and different strategies. For example, in their effort to avoid layoffs, one airline gave employees the opportunity to save their jobs by coming up with ways to work just as economically as the airline's outsourced workers did. Ticket clerks and other ramp-service personnel at seventeen of the airline's nineteen airports saved money—and retained their jobs—by redesigning their work schedules.

As another example, the senior management of an architecture engineering company upheld their Continuous Employment Commitment to employees by themselves taking temporary pay cuts during profit downturns. At another communications company, managers responded to an economic downturn with a particularly innovative plan, involving a 10 percent pay reduction offset by a 10 percent stock award. In addition, the company arranged with a brokerage firm to enable employees to sell their stock almost immediately upon issue. As another alternative, employees could defer their stock award for one year and as a result receive the stock at a discounted price and take advantage of its appreciation over the year-long period.

One company's Redeployment Program minimized the effects of the recent business downturn by placing approximately 90 percent of affected employees in other internal jobs. When a particular skill is no longer needed, employees enter a "redeployment pool" for three or four months. During that time, their full-time "job" is to find a new suitable position within the firm, through informational interviewing, enhancement classes to learn new skills, and other career development options. At the same time, they may take project work or training assignments within the company, without reducing their redeployment time. All these are examples of thinking innovatively about how to address an organization's needs, as well as your employees' needs.

As a final example, the sense of loss that comes with the post-merger breakup of a division was exercised at a unit of Glaxo Wellcome after the drug giant merged with competitor Smith-Kline Beecham. The 150-member Biomet team was broken up after a merger and reassigned to new teams. Before they moved on to new assignments, the large team met in a four-hour "wake" that gave all a chance to speak from the heart about their sadness, gratitude for colleagues, and their commitment to the search for better drugs. The ritual's format was a Native American "in council" circle composed of managers, scientists, and lab technicians who spoke as equals. No one was compelled to participate or attend, but all stayed for the entire ceremony. This was a creative and innovative way the managers addressed the sadness and sense of loss that employees experienced.

Manage Resistance by Providing a Sense of What's Next

Managers can often reduce the resistance to change by ensuring that employees have a sense of safety (i.e., they don't feel like the other shoe is yet to drop), and knowledge about what's coming next (i.e., how they can proactively exist in the changing environment). Both are effective counterweights to the natural human tendency to dig in your heels when things are changing.

Safety is the idea that employees will be supported throughout the change journey. It doesn't mean that there may not be difficult or hard choices that will need to be made, but it does mean that there is a sense of care with which the organization will pursue the change strategy, and that employees have all the information currently available. And knowledge of the immediate next step is really about helping employees understand what they can do to plug into the change; often employees are left wondering where the change or event leaves them ("what do I do now?"). Without creating that safety and awareness, you will be far more likely to encounter resistance and disengagement (caused by upset or frustration).

Cisco Systems works to smooth the transition for employees who join through mergers and acquisitions. All necessary office systems and equipment are up and running on the employee's first day. An orientation explains how to succeed in the Cisco culture, and how to use the company website for details about benefits and rules. And each employee is assigned a "sponsor" who acts as a mentor, not a boss. This practice really highlights the idea behind setting an employee up for success and giving them information about the very next step. Employees at Cisco Systems are likely to walk away thinking "I was thought of" or "I'm being supported here" as a result of such efforts.

145

We're All in This Together

The fifth and final aspect of your response template is to create a sense that everyone is facing the change together. Involving employees and providing the sense that "it's about us" and that everyone is a part of the whole can go a long way in addressing whatever disruptive events come your way. People tend to want to rally together and be a part of a community when something disruptive happens. So when the change occurs, look to create a sense of workplace community.

When Zappos changed locations in Las Vegas, they wanted to create a sense of community regarding the move. Tony Hsieh, the CEO, shared with us that "a little over a year ago, we announced we would be taking over Las Vegas City Hall [as our new offices]. . . . Because culture is so important, we want everyone under one roof and have land that we can expand upon. We surveyed employees about what they wanted in their dream workplace. We started thinking about other big campuses, like Nike or Google, and we realized that they were great for employees, but they were insular and didn't integrate with the community around them. We decided to take an NYU approach, where the campus blends with the city." Giving all of the employees a voice in the process and bringing them together—physically—was a way they communicated a sense of everyone being "in it together." Hsieh suggests that creating a sense of workplace community—especially as the company goes through a move—is good practice.

Jill Smart, the Chief HR Officer at Accenture, put the idea of "we're all in this together" in a different way. At Accenture, it's important for people to be agile and move when a disruptive event occurs. At Accenture, they moved from being a private partnership to a public company. Smart shared that "when we were a partnership, we did not have a focus on quarterly earnings like we do now. We started to really focus on the control that we're required to, but [that is] also good for us. Everybody just gets on board. We change fast. I think it's part of our culture, and that's just what we do." Certainly, it has taken Accenture some time to create a high-trust culture where speed and agility are hallmarks of how they work together, but Jill was able to point to several examples where employees did just that—jump in together and change to where the organization was moving.

At Devon Energy, Frank Rudolph, their Executive Vice President of HR, told us about a reduction in force they had to implement. When they did that, they knew that employees that were being let go would certainly be impacted, but they wanted to ensure that, even still, the entire Devon community was in it together. The executive leadership team agonized over how to make the transition easier on the employees affected by the situation. And so Devon Energy went out of their way to support the transition process of the employees being let go—as if they were a part of their community or family. Said Rudolph: "We put together packages for people that were above and beyond. They recognized that. It translates internally as more than 'they're doing the right thing.' It's almost like knowing that you're letting some family members go and you want to make sure that they do better than just land on their feet. That did happen. We tracked them all. It was about 84 percent of people landed in an equal or better-paying job without relocation. They had the executive team stand up in front of people and deliver the message. We delivered that message and we talked through it with people and we followed up and answered any question possible." For Devon Energy, it was important to underline that when change happens— regardless of who is impacted most—the change affects everyone and the company needs to focus on "being in it together."

There are scores of resources available to managers about how to deal with organizational change and manage resistance when changes occur. To be sure, the managers we spoke with know about many of these models and resources. But what was interesting from our point of view is that when a disruptive event occurs, managers at the best companies look at it as an opportunity to build trust. They use the moment to build a great workplace rather than think that the event precludes them from making an effort. Disruptive events will occur. That's the nature of organizational life today. The question for you as a manager is, How will you leverage the potential of your company's next disruptive event to create a high-trust culture?

WHAT TO DO NEXT

Disruptive events can provide an opportunity for you to create a great workplace. The first task in addressing disruptive events is to know that you can make a difference in how your employees experience the event. Consider the following ideas:

○ Disruptive events require you to communicate and check in more with your teams, not less. Find ways to reach out, even if it means just spending an extra sixty seconds checking in.

○ Involve employees wherever possible in thinking and problem solving. Involving them will go a long way to provide them a sense of security and what to expect going forward.

○ Before you go with the apparently easiest or quickest solution, consider other alternatives or options first.

○ Look for opportunities to celebrate or "pause" when a disruptive event occurs. What can be celebrated? How can you bring people together to reflect on or honor the present moment?

○ Remember to start from your strengths, and work from there.

CHAPTER 8

I'D BE A GREAT PEOPLE MANAGER IF IT WEREN'T FOR ALL THE PEOPLE

This book is aimed at helping you create a great workplace in order to leverage the talent and commitment of your people, and yet sometimes it seems that it's your people who *create* the obstacle to this very goal. This may be because of structural elements, like the impact of working in a union environment. Or it may be due to group characteristics, like overseeing a part-time labor force, or employees who demonstrate a sense of entitlement. As with the other areas we've covered, the "people challenge" is largely an issue borne of your approach. Instead of seeing people as an excuse, you must reframe the situation to see whatever obstacle you're given as an opportunity to enhance trust.

Sometimes you don't have a lot of control over the team you inherit when you become a supervisor. The team may have been newly formed prior to your arrival, or have been with the department for a very long time. You may have been a member of the team and then you were promoted, changing the relationship dynamics all of you had previously established. Or, in the

149

(hopefully) rare occasion, you may have been brought in to "shape up" an ineffective team. Still, while you may have inherited the players, it is important to not chalk up your lack of progress in shaping the culture to the lot of employees you were dealt. Doing so plays into the "external locus of control" thinking we discussed in Chapter 2. In other words, while you didn't select your team, it doesn't mean you don't have the power to create a great work environment with and for them.

Perhaps you work in a unionized environment where policies are governed by a union contract with your employees. Often, managers in these environments feel constrained, and share with us that because of union rules, they don't feel there's much they can do to change workplace culture. While a union contract may govern some key issues like pay, benefits, and performance management, our experience tells us that there is much that we *can* still do to build trust and create a great workplace.

One of the biggest "people" concerns we hear from managers is their fear of creating an entitlement mentality. The thinking goes that if you provide things for employees or start giving them extra perks, then there will be no end to it. Employees will continue to want more and more. Likewise, we sometimes hear that employees already seem to have an entitlement mentality, and the manager wants to know how to break out of that or deal with it. In one company we worked with, a manager confided to us, "These employees have it so good, and yet they continue to demand more. Where does it end?"

These challenges, as well as other "people" challenges, may actually exist, and as a manager, you need to find ways to address them. But these challenges point to a need for creative leadership rather than an excuse as to why a great work environment isn't possible. These apparent challenges are actually terrific opportunities to enhance the level of trust and create a more productive, healthy work environment. This chapter will show you how.

BUT MY TEAM'S MINDSET IS SO ENTRENCHED

When it comes to managing your team, you have to take into account a lot of information about the individuals in order to manage them effectively. Their motivation and commitment, job role and responsibilities, work history and expertise, and their family and life situation all factor in to how they show up each day and how they engage with you. Given your history with a particular employee, you may see patterns of behavior develop over time.

An individual's behavior may be driven by a variety of factors. For example, the behavior may be a part of a character trait (usual happiness) or a passing phase (sad because of a recent loss in the family) or a one-off event (confusion resulting from a work decision). We often say that "once is an anomaly; twice is a correlation; and three times is a pattern." A pattern of behavior is very different than a one-off behavior. And while both need to be addressed if the behavior is unproductive or counterproductive, your approach may be very different if it is a one-off behavior versus an ongoing pattern.

It's important when we notice a series of similar behaviors to avoid ascribing *motivation* or *assume* that this particular instance of behavior is part of a broader pattern. You may think to yourself when you see an employee acting a certain way, "Oh, that's just John being John." The assumption is that John's behavior is just a part of who he is as a person rather than based on a specific current circumstance. An example would be John's team thinking that his disorganization is just who he is rather than his responding to a work crisis that has changed his priorities. When you make this assumption, it also becomes easy to ascribe motive to those behaviors. The danger of this is that you lose the ability to see the behavior for what it is, as well as the ability to address

151

it. It is important to focus on the current situation and current behavior rather than externalize, contextualize, or explain away.

The only way to understand what is driving the behavior is to ask. You may believe that certain behaviors need to be modified or changed because they are getting in the way of that person being more successful. You can coach that person by taking the time to sit down with them and share that you have noticed a single behavior or pattern of behavior and wish to understand why. Only then can you understand the person's motivation. Then you can coach and develop the person from there. The point is to separate out why from what.

While your team and the individuals who compose it may be predetermined, what you do with the team is not. There is much you can do to influence the team if you focus on enhancing the level of trust, pride, and camaraderie. It is important, however, to set realistic goals. Influencing an individual's or team's behavior takes persistence and time. Set realistic milestones or goals for yourself, such as "I'll continue to show positive encouragement when Susie shows up on time, and to highlight how her timeliness supports our team effort."

A few years ago we consulted with a regional healthcare organization in the Midwest. Given their geographical community, they had low turnover and a majority of their employees had been there for years (if not decades). When a new CEO joined, he was faced with an entire organization seemingly entrenched in the thought pattern of "this is how we do things here." One very senior member of the nursing team, Alice, had been there for over thirty years, and had a habit of being mean-spirited to her staff. Her colleagues felt as though she was "set in her ways." She got results, however, so her behavior had always been "tolerated." The new CEO was clear that he wanted to develop a different type of work culture, and that such an attitude was counterproductive to his goals.

152

What would you do in this case? Fire Alice? Put her on warning? Perhaps provide her with a coach? Send her to training for interpersonal skills development? The CEO did none of those things. What he did do was spend time, and a lot of it, with her (and her staff and colleagues). Some of what he learned about her was that she had been through eight CEOs in her tenure, she had risen to a certain level in the organization and had "plateaued" (in her words). She had wanted to be a nurse since she was a little girl. Nursing was her one and only career; in a few short years, she would retire. Importantly, though she was known for her mean-spirited habits, she was also known for her dedication to her patients and her honesty with them.

"You have been here for thirty-eight years and are looking to retire in the next several years," the CEO said. "So what will your legacy be? And what do you *want* your legacy to be?" Alice had never really thought about that before, and when she did her answer was "I want my team to love the patients as much as I do." Now, you may be thinking that her "I'm the only one who cares" attitude is the very heart of the problem, but he tried to follow her logic. She went on to talk about her relationships with her patients. "I've known many of these people all my life," she said. "Sometimes, I see team members work with patients efficiently, but they don't see the whole story [behind the person]." In some ways, her response was surprising given her abrasive interactions her colleagues, but it gave him a window into why she behaved the way she did.

He told her that her idea was a noble one and had the promise of making the hospital a better place. But it could only happen if her team followed her model. "You're a leader if you have followers," he shared. "No one will follow you if they don't respect you enough to see what you see." While the change didn't happen all at once or in an easy manner—staff were wary and Alice sometimes struggled to behave in a manner consistent with her vision—when she retired recently, her team asked the board to start a "patient care award" in her name.

Three important points can be extracted from this story. First, the CEO made an interesting choice. He could have removed Alice from the organization, and that certainly would have sent a strong statement to everyone about his "meaning business." And likely, if things had not worked out, he may have addressed her behavior as a performance issue. But his initial inclination was not to approach it that way. Instead, he thought that the longer-term impact and message of keeping her would be much more aligned to his goal of creating a great workplace. This emphasizes the idea of hyperbolic discounting we discussed in Chapter 2; rather than take the short-term payoff, focus on the long-term goal.

The second point is that things *did* work out. His choice may have resulted in her continuing to behave in roughly the same way, and his efforts at creating a great workplace would appear weak or not very serious. Instead, he took a novel approach to addressing the issue by first understanding who Alice is as a person. A long-tenured employee, she had seen a lot of changes over her time at the hospital. She was getting closer to retirement so questions about impact, legacy, and her post-employment future were significant. And because of the hospital's location in a close-knit community, Alice knew many of the people who came through the hospital doors. She responded exactly as he had hoped.

The final point is that you have the team you have, and you need to begin from there. Sometimes you can choose the team you want, but quite often you can't. You need to refer back to the foundation of a great workplace and develop *relationships*, while building trust over time. Like the CEO in the story above, you are more likely to influence and have an impact in a high-trust environment than in a low-trust one. The most you will ever be able to do in a low-trust environment is order things to happen, and demand compliance. This works in the short term, but rarely in the long term.

BUT THE PEOPLE WHO WORK UNDER ME ARE SO *ENTITLED*

The idea of an "entitlement mentality" deserves attention in this book because the label itself serves as an excuse not to address the underlying behavior. Framing an issue or group of people as "entitled" certainly feels good and allows us to express our frustration, but does little to resolve it.

Entitlement is the belief that one is deserving of some sort of right or benefit, but is often used as a pejorative if there is no deeper framework or thinking process that underlies the right or benefit. Calling someone or something "entitled" is almost always done by the person or group who doesn't think the entitled party is deserving of that right or benefit.

The "entitlement mentality" in the workplace, then, refers to employees who behave as though they deserve some right, benefit, perk, or special treatment. They may feel as though they have earned it, or conversely, that they don't have to put in the same effort or follow the same rules as others (usually their forebears). Managers tend to think that this mentality is due to an employee's tenure, position, performance, or previous work arrangement. When we talk to managers about creating a great workplace, we sometimes hear concern that treating employees well will lead to them being too comfortable or expecting more and further benefits or perks.

Two connected issues here need to be examined. First, what rights or benefits ought to be due to employees, and for what purposes or reasons? If you are trying to create a great workplace culture, then how should you think about your "psychological contract" with employees and what you provide them? In its most basic form, a psychological contract is an individually and implicitly held understanding about what is required in their employment relationship, and what they should receive in return. For example, a job applicant who is told "We provide a lot of flexibility for our people" would expect to find that his job provides for a degree of latitude in terms of schedule, work flow, or control, even if it is not explicitly stated in the employee handbook. Employees may have developed a belief that a workplace will provide certain benefits or rights because, simply, someone at the company said it would or implied it would.

Every employee has a "psychological contract" with their organization. It often starts before the employee arrives, and it becomes further nuanced over time based on the actions of the organization, and if widely held, it may even become a part of an organization's culture and identity. An organization that we worked with had never had a single layoff of employees in its 160-year history. In the 2000–2001 economic downturn, the company made a painful decision to reduce its workforce. It struck employees particularly hard, as they had come to expect that the firm would never do such a thing. Thirteen years later, the "dark days" still routinely come up in conversation with employees, and it has changed the way these employees think about job security and stability.

Once you understand the role of psychological contract as it relates to entitlement, your second concern should be how to manage when what is expected in terms of rights or benefits is not enough, or too much. Further, consider the confusion and reactionary indignation that happens when the rights or benefits are not aligned with the culture, or if employees use the stated goal of creating a great workplace to demand greater or different rights or benefits.

As a leader, part of your responsibility is to understand the nature of the psychological contract your employees have with the organization along with what is included in this understanding and why. In great workplaces, the organization invests a great deal of energy and thought into articulating what they believe about the nature of employees and the workplace. And this should override any egregious misconceptions on the part of employees. For example, are employees to be trusted, or controlled and managed? Is work to be performed at a certain place and time, or is the focus on results and work can be performed anywhere and at any time? Such beliefs give rise to certain values and cultural anchors, which frame the types of practices and programs that are offered.

As an example, at Whole Foods Market, leaders believe that having a sense of community is important—both between employees and with customers. Such a belief fosters a sense that all of the employees are "in it together." And this in turn gives rise to such practices as bonuses (or gain sharing) based on team goals rather than individual goals. At Whole Foods, their practices are aligned with what employees have come to expect, and if there are any changes to be made, then the company carefully considers how to communicate that in such a way that the psychological contract is renegotiated, rather than breached.

If you are working to create a great workplace in your team, department, or organization, then you will be well served by thinking about the nature of work, its meaning to your employees, and your fundamental beliefs about what motivates and engages employees. How do such beliefs shape your work values and approach to how you supervise and manage? And finally, what are the types of policies, practices, and programs you would choose to implement that align to these beliefs and values? The answers to these questions form the basis of your psychological contract. It is when we lavish employees with benefits without couching them as part of a larger agreement that benefits the organization that the issue of "entitlement mentality" often arises.

Thus, if you find that your practices and programs are not aligned with your fundamental beliefs, then either what you are offering implicitly to employees will create outsized expectations on the part of employees, or real frustration and disappointment on the part of your team (and maybe even high turnover). Perks and benefits are good only if they are in service of supporting your workplace culture and goals. When your employees come to expect more than what is provided, then it is clear that the psychological contract is misaligned. You may need to step back and course correct with your team. It is useful to discuss with them *why* something exists or does not exist. Providing that additional context can sometimes address the misalignment, and also serves the useful purpose of supporting employees' understanding of the organization's values and cultural identity. Also, know that while beliefs seldom change, workplace practices will change over time. Organizations are dynamic and interact with the external environment (as when changes need to be made to healthcare benefits because of external costs or regulations). So, when you change a practice like your firm's "telecommuter policy" and your employees have come to rely upon it, you will need to have a careful plan in place, over-communicate it, and engage employees on the change.

BUT MY EMPLOYEES ARE ALL A PART OF A UNION—MY HANDS ARE TIED

First, a little background on unions. Trade or labor unions are the legally recognized representatives of workers in many industries in the United States and around the world. The union bargains with the employer on behalf of its members for certain pay, benefits, and work rules. "Works councils" are a local complement to such unions in Europe. Unions began in the nineteenth century as a response to the economic impact of the industrial revolution. In the United States, labor unions saw an increase in participation through the 1950s, but the number of employees involved has dwindled to less than 15 percent in recent times. Representation of workers in other countries, however, remains strong; in a 2010 survey, 70 percent of employees in Finland reported belonging to a union.[1]

While unions enjoy strong support in Europe and in many countries, attitudes have changed in the United States over time. According to a recent Gallup survey, unions still enjoy public support, although Americans' likelihood to say they approve of them has declined. Currently, 58 percent of Americans say they approve of unions, while 33 percent disapprove. A slight majority, 52 percent, say they've tended to sympathize with unions in labor disputes over the last two or three years, while 34 percent say they've sympathized with the companies.[2] However, actual union membership has declined to a ninety-seven-year low of 11.3 percent, according to the Bureau of Labor Statistics.[3] In any given year, about twenty or so of the one hundred best companies on the *FORTUNE* list have employees represented by a union. These firms vary in industry and size and overall union representation, but the role of unions is an important factor in their work environment. Leaders in these organizations have placed a focus on creating trust between "workers" and "management" as a winning strategy. This certainly underscores our contention that any company can be a great workplace, and that you can create a great workplace regardless of union status.

In organizations that have unionized employees, a formal negotiated contract governs and frames the employer-employee relationship. The terms and conditions of employment and working conditions are drawn up in the contract, which is legally

159

binding. If a dispute occurs between an employee and employer, then a grievance process provided for in the contract is usually followed. If the issue cannot be resolved, then it is usually resolved through arbitration. If this arrangement characterizes your workplace, then the contract probably governs what is and is not permissible in terms of worker rights and working conditions. For example, the union contract governs the performance evaluation system, bonuses, survey employee attitudes, and so on. It can seem as if the agreement constrains your ability as a manager to change the working arrangements or conditions of your team. While this is essentially true, we find that managers use the labor contract as a crutch or excuse for not creating a great workplace. The truth is, unions are not a valid excuse—a manager can still create a great workplace in a unionized environment.

In the previous section we discussed the idea of the psychological contract as it relates to the "entitlement mentality." Whether an organization has a clearly articulated employment contract, like the ones developed between employers and unions, all employees have a "psychological contract" with organizations. This psychological contract is only loosely defined as a "contract" because it is rarely articulated unless there is a perceived breach, and usually not mutually understood. However, it exists, and it is shaped by the employer in terms of the hiring process and employment offer, the human resource policies, and the expectations of managers. Think of the psychological contract as an additional layer on top of the actual union contract.

How might you navigate both types of contracts in order to create a great workplace? First, it is important to recall that it is not *what* you do as much as *how* you do it, and better to treat every interaction with employees as an opportunity to build trust. As an example of this, consider American Cast Iron Pipe Co. (ACIPCO) of Birmingham, Alabama, which has included employees in company decisions since 1924. Not too long ago, the employees

160

voted to replace the seventy-year-old cafeteria facility, knowing that the funds would come from "their money"—cash flow that could be used for wages or bonuses. An employee committee researched other company cafeterias in the region, designed the new ACIPCO dining space, selected the contractor, and submitted the plan to management. It was the act of involving employees in the decision-making process here that supported the company's effort at maintaining a great workplace.

The other thing to remember is that having a union does not absolve you of your responsibility to develop a trusting relationship with employees. In fact, sometimes your organization can lead in this regard. Take Graniterock Construction. They were the first company in the construction industry to introduce performance-based pay, and still one of a few unionized companies in any industry to expand performance-based pay to include the collective bargaining agreements with its five unions. They didn't accept that the union contract prevented them from doing this; rather they figured out the best pay system and then incorporated it into the contract. Graniterock's Individual Professional Development Plan (IPDP) includes thirty-six salary ranges, each of which has five compensation levels (and quarter steps within levels). These ranges are based on industry salary studies, and are reviewed annually by the Executive Committee. These IPDP ranges make it possible to objectively determine compensation levels based on an analysis of each individual's job knowledge and demonstrated on-the-job skills. Because the IPDP is clearly defined and organized, transparent (based on industry studies), and underscores a sense of fairness regarding compensation, it enhanced the level of trust at Graniterock.

At the more local team level you can meet regularly with your local union representative to discuss upcoming projects and opportunities, and mutually decide how best to collaborate in order to benefit employees and the organization. For example, each hotel in the Toronto-based Four Seasons Hotels chain maintains a "Direct Line Committee" of employees from each department, including union representatives (or stewards). The committee meets alone with the General Manager every month for an open and honest exchange of views. Like the GMs at Four Seasons, start with developing one relationship (with the union representative) and go from there. In this way, the managers and the union use their arrangement to strengthen bonds and communication and to work more closely together, not less.

BUT THE CHARACTERISTICS OF MY WORKFORCE JUST DOESN'T MAKE IT POSSIBLE

Many managers we've worked with have said the nature of the employment relationship presents a challenge to creating a great workplace. Part-time employees, or a contract, temporary, or contingent workforce presents its own list of challenges and obstacles. For example, some managers suggest that having temporary workers lessens the commitment to the organization's goals and objectives. Part-time workers can pose challenges because the recruitment, selection, and onboarding of these employees is sometimes less rigorous. They can also seem to be less committed if they are juggling several different jobs. But here again, this need not be an impediment to creating a great workplace.

As an example of this, Balfour Beatty is a multinational engineering and construction management firm, and a *FORTUNE* 100 best company. We sat down with Robert Van Cleave, the U.S. Chairman and CEO, and a group of managers to talk about how they work with the various subcontractors to complete their construction projects. Robert shared, "We've got about 3,000 salaried employees and about 1,000 hourly/craft workers. We have Ph.D.s, superintendents, accountants, specialty construction workers in the field, and everything in between. Everyone has a level of respect for what needs to get accomplished. Either individually or as the business leader, you cast your shadow, and the way you cast your shadow across a subcontractor community is talked about and seen, and people respond to it." Everyone counts . . . and in other words, subcontractor employee teams are included in the Balfour "workplace" in terms of safety, engagement, accountability, and company culture. One of the managers at Balfour Beatty added to Van Cleave's comments: "I noticed right away that our safety culture is shared with subcontractors. From the moment you step on site, it's all about safety, health, and well-being—or what we call Zero Harm. I've heard the same thing back from the subcontractors." In other words, subcontractors instantly understand their value to Balfour Beatty as human beings, subcontractor or not. Another manager said that "safety can give the impression that you are just trying to limit your liability. Our culture here shows that we actually care for each and every worker, regardless of whether they are with the biggest subcontractor or smallest subcontractor. We want to ensure that each and every one of those employees goes home to their family every day. Everybody here buys into that. What I hear the most when I have a dialogue with a subcontractor is that they feel we truly care about their employees, care about them getting paid, care about their financial stability, care about them doing well. I hear that over and over and over."

These managers also see how the subcontractors are part of the value chain. If they're a part of providing value to the client, then it serves Balfour well to ensure that they're also seen as an extension of their organization and its culture. The managers at Balfour Beatty point to several useful lessons for us in working with people who are part-time, contract, or contingent. First, understand that they *are* an important part of your business and

163

let them know they make a difference. Since they may not be with your organization for a long time, it's important that they see the impact of their work.

Second, it is useful to solicit their feedback and involve them in the life of the business. The Balfour Beatty manager regularly asks for and receives feedback from the subcontractors; that's how he knows the subcontractors appreciate the company's attentiveness to safety. And third, pay attention to your "shadow," as Robert Van Cleave suggests. Other employees, both full-time and part-time (or contingent), are watching the level of respect with which you engage these workers. You can demonstrate that respect by ensuring they receive a full orientation to your organization, are equipped with the appropriate training and resources to do their job, and provided appropriate transition services (or a proper "thank you") at the end of their service.

BUT MY WORKFORCE IS *YOUNG*—THEY DON'T CARE ABOUT A COHESIVE WORKPLACE CULTURE

Organizational diversity is sometimes viewed as an obstacle to creating a great place to work. The wide-ranging needs and perspectives that people from different backgrounds bring to an organization can often be viewed as difficult because of the inherent complexity. Issues of race, gender, education, age, ability, nationality, religious orientation, or sexual orientation might all play out in the work environment. But here again, your people are not the obstacle. Indeed, best companies look for opportunities to create an inclusive work environment that leverages the talent of their people and uses that energy and creativity to enhance the bottom line. In this brief section, we focus on one specific aspect of diversity: millennial workers (those born between

1980 and 2000). The lessons for managers can be more broadly applied to other aspects of diversity.

Recently we talked with a manager at a large telecommunications firm—let's call him Alexander. His department included thirty IT professionals and his team was from around the world. "I'm not sure you can create a great place to work in this environment," he offered. "It seems like I have everything working against me. The IT field is difficult, as is the telecommunications industry. I have a virtual team, spread around the world. They are from a bunch of different countries and most of them are young guys and this is their first job out of college. The challenges are too great here." We certainly sympathize with his experience, but as you know by now, there simply is no good excuse.

Alexander's apparent challenges stem from his belief that workforce diversity can result in insurmountable obstacles. Having such a diverse team increases the complexity in terms of communication, coordination, collaboration, and perceptions of fairness. Creating a great place to work *is* work, no doubt, but armed with accurate information and a realistic perspective on how to advance his goals, Alexander can do much good in service of creating a high-trust work environment.

We'll leave Alexander's concerns about the IT and telecommunications fields aside for now, as we already covered the industry excuse in Chapter 6. Let's instead focus on the challenge of generational differences in the workplace in particular. A diverse employee population supports creativity and innovation, but it is also important to manage it well in order to harness such benefits. In most organizations, managers focus on ensuring adequate representation or fostering programs that promote diversity, which are necessary, but not sufficient.

The majority of best companies have a clear strategy for creating an inclusive, multicultural work environment. Perhaps your organization isn't one that has diversity as a core value or a clear strategy as yet. However, like Alexander, you have a diverse workforce and you wish to create an inclusive culture that values what employees bring to the workplace. Consider Accenture then, and what one of their leaders, Jill Smart, shares about the diversity that generational differences bring.

Jill is realistic and understands that there are real challenges to dealing with generational differences in the workplace. But there are also really great opportunities. Jill shared with us that "some people will be negative about the younger generations and their demands and their expectations and their lack of work ethic. . . . The negative of having to deal with different generations for me is that it makes my job a lot harder because different generations have different demands and expectations and want to be communicated with in different ways. One guy is never going to read his email and the other guy is never going to check his text messages."

On the other hand, Jill says that "the positive is that the younger generation that's demanding more balance and demanding that we contribute to the community and have corporate citizenship and the environment as a priority, how could that be a bad thing? If they want more work/life balance, somehow, I'm going to eventually get more balance, too. The demands that they have are good. I think taking advantage of the differences in the generations can really work to our advantage as a company." Jill opens the door for rethinking what the younger generation might bring.

If you are in the fortunate position of having a workforce as diverse as Alexander's, consider it a real opportunity for learning and innovation. It can be a creative strength that supports the development of trust. Seen in this light, Accenture has something useful to teach us: Diversity and generational diversity are vehicles that support the creation of a great workplace environment.

WHAT TO DO NEXT

In sum, your people may appear to sometimes be the actual obstacle getting in the way of creating a great workplace. However, this is really not the case. Going forward:

○ Your people may have very strongly held beliefs or opinions about the organization or the workplace. Listen to them and help them make connections to the value of creating a great workplace.

○ Be creative and innovative in addressing people's needs, interests, and self-concept.

○ If you are experiencing an "entitlement mentality," it is likely a function of built-up expectations. Talk about it with your team. Make them understand that while practices might change in order to respond to the external environment, fundamental values and beliefs are unlikely to change.

○ Having a union doesn't let you off the hook—you still need to find ways to develop trust-based relationships with your people. Collaborate with union leadership, rather than avoid and antagonize.

○ Union members look carefully at how you treat them versus non-union members. A fundamental respect and sense of fairness, regardless of union affiliation, will go a long way to earning the necessary credibility.

○ Rather than get frustrated (or confused) at the behavior of millennials (or other diverse groups for that matter), understand that they bring specific gifts and traits to the workplace. They might help all of us think more broadly about how work can be effectively accomplished.

167

CHAPTER 9

MY BOSS ATE MY
HOMEWORK

Gentle readers, we've finally reached a point in our discussion where we will ultimately say to you, "You're right. We've never seen a company like that become a great place to work." That is, we've never seen an organization reach, or even approximate, its potential as a workplace of trust, pride, and camaraderie without the buy-in of top leaders.

Lack of leader support is wearisome, as we know all too well. After our talks with leaders who don't "get it," we feel fatigued and dejected. In contrast, after we've talked with leaders who do get it, we feel buoyed and delighted. But there is much that can be done to create a great workplace before you throw in the towel. First, consider why your leaders don't get it. Do they know the importance of a great workplace? Do they care? Or do they believe they are doing the right thing when the reality is that they are not? We agree with famed German writer and intellectual Johann Wolfgang von Goethe, who wrote in 1774: "Misunderstandings and neglect create more confusion in this world than trickery and malice. At any rate, the last two are certainly much less frequent." In other words, perhaps your leaders *can* be persuaded, if you can help them understand and act. We'll discuss ways to help you persuade them.

Even if you never actually set foot in the sphere of influence with your organization's executives, you can create a great workplace in your own department. This we *have* seen, many times over. In virtually every organization with which we have worked, there are departments, divisions, and locations where employees have a great workplace experience, despite the average experience of others in the organization. When we first began to observe this, we asked pointed questions to discover what was different about those managers. Were they more skilled? Did they have advantages over others with regard to budget, location, or nature of the work? Did they somehow operate outside the culture of the rest of the organization? With very few exceptions, the answer was, in a word, "no."

Here's what we found was true: Managers in these departments created a sense of identity in their own department, an essential component of a great workplace we described in Chapter 3. They also adopted a healthy mindset, largely devoid of the cognitive obstacles we summarized in Chapter 2. They worked hard to overcome the real challenges facing their work group. But that doesn't mean their road was easy. As tough as it is to maintain a great workplace over time, it is even more difficult to do so when your work group is an oasis of great in a sea of mediocrity.

Nonetheless, within your work group, you do have a modicum of control, and we'll talk about how to use it wisely. We'll help you understand and address the challenges of doing so without top leader support. We'll also discuss how to influence others such that your task becomes easier. We'll conclude this chapter by giving you some straight talk about your role as an employee (rather than simply a manager) in your organization, and how to manage if your boss is in the camp of misunderstanding and neglect when it comes to your own workplace experience.

THE IGNORANT LEADER EXCUSE

It is difficult to imagine a leader in today's world who isn't acutely aware of the need to create a workplace that attracts and develops top talent. Some believe we're about to face a labor shortage, while some do not. In reality, it hardly matters, because the fact remains that most HR professionals put at the top of their list the need to attract and retain educated, dedicated, and resourceful employees.[1] Moreover, most leaders recognize diversity matters, and not just in the traditional way that speaks of headcounts, but in real, meaningful ways that affect the way teams succeed. Just as Great Place to Work® Institute did several years ago, Diversity, Inc., a leader in educating employers about the business benefits of diversity, now recognizes the top fifty companies each year that embrace inclusive environments through their programs, policies, and practices. Last but not least, we see that consumers too look for organizations that treat their employees well. Witness the rise of the B-Corporation, a legal designation available in some states that allows organizations to balance the concerns of shareholders with those of employees, the community, and the environment. And these are just a few of the signposts that show the importance of a top-notch, diverse, and socially responsible workforce to business success.

Given the weight of the evidence in their environment, let's assume that your top leaders are aware of the need to create a great workplace, but they don't have a handle on what it looks like in your company, in your industry, or in your country. It goes without saying that they haven't read this book—maybe they don't read! But, it is likely that visible examples of a great workplace exist right under their noses.

Enter positive deviance, the notion that workable models of the workplace we find so elusive are often already in existence. Said another way, if a small group of managers in your company, within your industry, and within your country has done something right, learn from them. Seek them out, ask them for some time, and start a conversation about their practices and how they overcome the same obstacles you may be facing. Don't be surprised if they haven't realized they have something to teach. If they already have the great workplace mindset we discussed in Chapter 2, they may not realize the countless things they do to create their desirable work environment. Likewise, if you are that manager who has created a great workplace in your own department or division, you may just be the deviant that your leader needs to know about. At the very least, your fellow managers need to know about your success. Start roundtables or discussion boards, perhaps informally at first. But, as best practice sharing gains momentum, you may model practices we found at the many organizations we visited. Best practice sharing is perhaps the easiest and the most acceptable way to engage in sharing and learning through positive deviance. Indeed, when you hear Ceree Eberly, Chief People Officer at The Coca-Cola Company, talk about it, it seems not only easy to share best practices, it is a business imperative. "We have over 700,000 employees in our worldwide bottling system and approximately 150,000 employees within the company itself. We're not going to do everything the same way, but we're sharing best practices related to employee insights, best-place-to-work strategies, common frameworks around talent management and capabilities." She went on to say that doing so leverages Coca-Cola's institutional knowledge, leads to new discovery, and systematically helps the organization avoid duplication. Richard Pascale, co-author of *The Power of Positive Deviance*, notes that sharing insights from successful subunits is an exercise in leading from the bottom-up, because it is often the people in unlikely places who have devised solutions to problems that seem complex from a top-down perspective.[2] But he also notes that there must be a desire on the part of others to find a solution to a complex problem. That brings us to our next leader problem: when he is neglectful.

THE NEGLECTFUL LEADER EXCUSE

Even more frustrating than uneducated leaders are the cavalier leaders who see the workplace as a concern separate from the fundamentals of financial health, profitability, and market leadership. The workplace is not simply where business happens, it is *how* business happens, and the health of the relationships in the organization translate into more productivity, efficiency, and innovation, which in turn lead to more measurable outcomes. The problem is, we cannot quantify the ways in which the workplace culture matters, or at least in the very direct way we can quantify error rates, sales growth, and turnaround time. Thus, it is easier to drive change in these more tangible metrics rather than in workplace culture, and those metrics become the accepted truth as to what drives business success.

While imperfect, becoming fluent about the metrics that do exist is important in order to speak the language of the neglectful leader. Every year, Great Place to Work® Institute reports on the financial health of the publicly traded companies on the list, and every year, they show that organizations with trust, pride, and camaraderie outperform their peers. Moreover, intermediary metrics such as turnover and absenteeism further support our claim that a great workplace matters.

But there is still a basic faith that top leaders must have in the importance of culture to business success that we wish was more widespread. Without this fundamental belief in its importance, culture isn't seen as a part of the leadership role, because it will never be easily quantified. Informing your leader that other leaders hold this basic belief (particularly when those leaders hail from successful companies) is another way you might help him see the connection.

CEO of Devon Energy, John Richels, spoke to us at length about culture's importance, despite its elusiveness. He starts with a response to an excuse we hear often: "Culture is the warm and fuzzy stuff, not the stuff of bottom-line business results." Richels counters, "We don't do this because we're all nice guys; it's not for altruistic purposes. We do it because we fundamentally believe that a happy, challenged, motivated workforce puts forth more effort, commitment, and energy, which translates to better bottom-line results." Frank Rudolph, Devon's Executive Vice President of HR, took Richels' thoughts one step further and illustrated that the payoff follows the belief that the workplace makes a difference, sometimes in unexpected ways. "Take something like wellness that's perceived as being soft," he illustrated. "We built a wellness center based on all the data that was out nationally. To our surprise, we showed that you can take a squishy area like wellness and when you launch that initiative, your highly engaged workforce that trusts management will jump in. We have 1,300 people signed up and 80 percent of them are regular users. We decreased healthcare costs by $5 million in two years. It's netting a great result."

Oftentimes, the first organizations in a given sector whose leaders adopt the idea that culture matters reap the benefits of being a leader in the industry. One manager at Balfour Beatty remembered it this way. "I think for a long time we had old-school thought around what construction was. That may have been applicable fifteen or twenty years ago, but now, especially with our focus on meeting the client's ultimate needs and partnering with them to understand their business, construction as an exercise merely in meeting time and budget doesn't work. It's exciting to think about what we can be, as a service and value provider, even above meeting the basic building needs of our construction contract."

At some point, having a great workplace will be a necessity for success rather than a competitive advantage that can be dismissed as one of many options to pursue. Co-founder of Great Place to Work® Institute, Robert Levering wrote in 2012 that "today most companies see being a great workplace as optional or a low priority. But as more and more companies become great workplaces, a tipping point will be reached. And the pressures from employees, customers, and investors will create a world where creating a great workplace will be the norm, not the exception."

As exciting as it may be for managers in companies where their leaders begin to care about the health of the workplace, there is no magic solution we can share with you about how to get them there. What we can say, though, is that the trend in most industries is to embrace culture as a key pillar in the organization's success. In other words, hang in there—times are changing. Investors are sitting up to take notice, and leaders are attributing their organization's very survival to their workplace.

One of those trendsetters is John Mackey, Co-CEO of Whole Foods Market. In his book *Conscious Capitalism* with Raj Sisodia, he writes: "A company that today has over $11 billion in sales annually would have died in its first year if our stakeholders hadn't loved and cared about us—and they wouldn't have loved and cared for us if we had not been the kind of business we were."[3] In other words, it's not just shareholders who matter in the financial picture, but employees, customers, and suppliers. Indeed, anyone who has a relationship with the company affects its financial picture. Leaders who "get it," like Mackey, are beginning to

175

talk more directly about it. A healthy culture will soon no longer be a luxury; it will be a mandate.

Until that time, what's a manager to do under a neglectful leader? As we suggested with the ignorant leader, be the positive deviant. Secondly, never pass up an opportunity to educate and remind your leaders on the benefits of creating a healthy workplace culture. Even once they've been recognized for their workplace, leaders in best companies keep it top of mind. Gwen McDonald, the Executive Vice President of Human Resources at NetApp, agrees. "'Great Place to Work' is in everything we talk about, and every leader talks about it. It's contagious. It's not something that's ad hoc or an afterthought. It's part of the DNA of our company. Every manager recognizes it, whether it's been explicitly expressed or they've observed it." You can be that voice at your organization. At the very least, you'll be able to make sure leaders are not acting from a place of ignorance about what is possible. Third, act as if you work at a great workplace. Sometimes acting "as if" is just the catalyst needed to get where you want to go. Even if doing so feels like beating your head against a wall when talking to people outside of the work group, department, or division you lead, you can certainly make headway in your own area of responsibility.

THE WEIGHT OF THE WORLD EXCUSE

Some managers don't see their leader's ignorance or neglect as the obstacle; rather, it is the sheer energy required to create a great work *group* in the midst of a mediocre organization that keeps them stuck. To those managers, we say that in addition to seeing great work groups in mediocre companies, we've also seen lackluster work groups in great companies. Therefore, your excuse doesn't work on us. Your role as a manager matters, and while much of your success is inextricably related to the support you receive from the organization, just as much (if not most) of your success rests upon your shoulders alone.

We've written a lot about the importance of relationships in this book, and now it's time to bring it full circle. Managers create the relationships through which employees experience much of their organizational life, and without trust in them, any goodwill created at higher levels in the organization just won't make the same impact.

One manager at NetApp emphasized the importance of taking personal responsibility for creating a great workplace. "It's not that hard," he said. "It all comes down to interpersonal interactions. I had a job out of college and one boss was great. That boss went away and a new boss came in, and I hated the job. I was doing the exact same stuff, but the boss made the difference."

Everything we've discussed so far is scalable to the size of your work group. The sense of organizational identity we discussed in Chapter 3 can be reframed as the sense of identity for your work group. Your pool of administrative assistants isn't there to meet the needs of busy realtors; they're the directors of first impressions, as they're called at Baptist Health South Florida. Your customer service staff isn't there to be a repository of complaint and frustration; they help people solve problems, or as in the case of Zappos' customer service staff, they create happiness. Your retail employees don't just ring up sales, they help people get outside, as they do at REI. Even if your organization doesn't have a good handle on how groups of employees provide value, our guess is that you do.

All of the cognitive errors we discussed in Chapter 2 apply no matter your position in the organization. You are susceptible to an external locus of control, believing that other departments in your organization are lucky or charmed. While they may have different challenges, they are challenged too, and your job is to

177

adopt an internal locus of control such that you believe you can make changes that make a difference. You are also responsible for believing your department will become a great workplace in its own way and on its own timeline, and that it has the potential to exceed any expectations that you can possibly adopt for it. Your attitude as a manager is important to your employees' experience of a great workplace. Finally, throughout the other chapters of the book, we've illustrated common challenges that may seem to be a function of an organization rather than a department, but you don't need to make an impossible leap to realize that differences in industries are akin to differences to functional areas, and events often rattle one department more than they do others.

That's the recap of how what we've already covered is relevant no matter who your leader is. Now let's move forward. What else can you do, personally, if your leaders haven't embraced the view that a great workplace is a strategic imperative? We've broken it into three guidelines: 1) use your resources and authority, 2) work with the decisions your leaders make, not against them, and 3) focus on the how rather than the what.

Use Your Resources and Authority

One more time: If you can build a relationship, you can create a great workplace. Therefore, you have all the resources you need. In other words, resources—in this case—do not translate to money or authority. And unlike most organizational resources, they are self-replenishing. As one manager at NetApp told us, "When it comes down to the matter of managing a staff, I take that as a first priority. If there's an issue or if there's recognition that I have to give out, I take care of that first. The work stuff comes after that. Employees see that it is my priority and they start making it a priority for themselves." Great workplaces are about everyone, not just the manager. In essence, your relationship with people is the only resource you need—and it is renewable. That is, the more you build the relationship, the more your employees will meet you halfway. Said more directly, if you pave the way for making trust, pride, and camaraderie a priority, your people will too.

It may be true that your work group is the only area of the organization in which you can exercise a great deal of influence over the organizational environment. But CEOs of great workplaces know that their success depends upon you. John Richels of Devon Energy was frank about this point. "We have found in exit interviews that what's so important to people is the relationship with their immediate supervisor. I can do anything I want and set any example that I want to as the leader of the organization, but if the direct supervisors aren't doing the same thing, it becomes very difficult for people to believe in the organization and what it's all about." Just as Stephen Covey suggested in his seminal work *The Seven Habits of Highly Effective People,* you need to focus intently on those things that you can influence, because they are the only things you can do anything about.[4] In so doing, your sphere of influence expands—perhaps by granting you the credibility and social currency to gain an audience with your top leaders about the importance of the workplace.

Work with Decisions from the Top

Even in organizations with benevolent, principled, and mission-driven leaders who place priority on the workplace, managers are sometimes faced with mandates that don't fold seamlessly into the operations of their own work group. Especially in times of rapid growth, top leaders may need to standardize policy in order to gain efficiencies and more accurate metrics. External forces put pressure on leaders to make cuts and freeze expenditures, new

179

laws and regulations require organizational restructuring and reporting requirements, and the list goes on. If you do make people a priority, decisions from the top that don't align with that priority may seem at odds with your efforts. But in the best companies, we see managers taking a different approach.

First and foremost, they are authentic about things that need to get done in order to accomplish larger goals. One manager at Whole Foods Market illustrated this by saying, "I'll tell my team members that I know nobody wants to do [a certain task], but it has to get done. It's the honesty that matters. Somebody doesn't have to pretend that they like a task that they don't like. They can just be who they are and do the job and know that they're going to get to do something else another day." Managers who try to sugarcoat blatantly annoying tasks, or pretend as if every assignment should be treated with gratitude don't build trust easily with their employees for two reasons. One is that doing so dismisses the feelings of the employee, which also dismisses any hope of their being seen as a person and not just a hired hand. The other reason trust falters is that the employee is left with the perception that the manager isn't being honest. It's okay to express concerns about an assignment, as long as those concerns are paired with a rededication to a larger sense of purpose.

Another manager from Whole Foods Market also supported the recommendation for authenticity, and added that a call to action is also needed. "I find that transparency is really important. Of course, if you're middle management, you're not going to just blurt out whatever you feel about your boss in that moment to your team members. But you can say, 'Here's the deal. We've been given this job and if you want to moan and groan about it, then let's get it out of our system. Then let's figure out how we can support each other to make this happen.' It's working *with* your team, because sometimes that's all you have. You've got to lead, you've got to be there, and you've got to listen and support through whatever is going on."

At Teach for America, managers take the same approach. One of them told us, "You want to create a culture of transparency so that your team knows that when they ask you a direct question, you give them a direct answer and that you operate with compassion and empathy. If something's not a great situation, call it. You say it's not great and provide context. You explain what you can do together to make it better. My role as a leader is to help make meaning for people on our team and to help ensure alignment across a very large organization."

The desired approach is necessarily complex. Be authentic, honest, and forthright with your people about the negative aspects of what you are required to do. But then be solution focused, and use the requirement as an opportunity to band together and create wild success. One without the other is less likely to lead to a great workplace environment.

Exercise Your Right to the "How"

Working with top leadership decisions rather than against them is a specific example of a broader recommendation we've mentioned before: Focus on how you do what you do more than what you do. You may not have a lot of choice in what you do. But you do have a choice in how you do it. If you must conduct performance reviews once per year, the support you provide people in those meetings is what will create a strong sense of trust. If you must staff your department at a certain level, collaborating with employees as to how to meet that standard is what helps employees feel respected. You get the idea. Top leaders can direct much of *what* you do, but *how* you do it is up to you.

181

The guiding rule, as we discussed at the outset of the book, is to treat every interaction as an opportunity to build trust. Or take it one step simpler, and see people as people. One manager we spoke with at Balfour Beatty Construction learned this lesson early in his career. "I was working late one night, and I started a conversation with the cleaning people. They told me there was a really nice guy in the front office. I went up there and it was the CEO! He was working away but he treated everyone, including the cleaning people like they were the President of the company too. He treated them with respect. If you treat everyone like someone, whether it is a subcontractor, a client, or a member of the cleaning staff, they will feel respected and engaged, and ultimately do a better job because they are happier in the workplace." That last point—keeping employees happy—should matter, whether or not you believe your actions affect your work group's performance and ultimately the bottom line. Taking the time to connect with people as individuals rather than checkpoints in an elaborate process flow is worth it, if for no other reason than it keeps you focused on the reason you're there in the first place—to facilitate your employees' success and well-being. And doing so doesn't mean enlarging your current role. "I don't think it takes that much extra effort," said a manager at NetApp. "I can deliver the same exact message to you two different ways, and one way is going to sound good and one way is going to sound bad. It can be positive news or constructive news. I am in charge of the messaging, and either approach I take is not going to take much more effort on my part."

One manager we coached, Aaron Littleman, certainly felt the weight of his mediocre company. He had long ago dismissed any hope to change things beyond his immediate work group. In fact, a job search was on the horizon, after the kids were grown and his wife finished graduate school. But, in the meantime, he was dedicated to creating the best work experience possible for his employees. He took the time to coach and mentor them, knowing it would help them to find jobs if they also desired a change. He made sure they had the resources they needed to do the best job they could, and showed appreciation for a job well done. While Aaron ran a great deal of interference between his team and leadership, he also was honest with his employees. Eventually, Aaron will leave his organization, but he has stayed longer than either one of us thought possible. His higher purpose, a great workplace for his employees, has been quite rewarding despite the machinations of the leadership in his organization.

If you're working diligently to create a great workplace even though your leaders aren't working so diligently, we applaud you. You are the unsung heroes of employees everywhere, not just in your own organization. Whether you know it or not, you are adding to the groundswell of momentum that will lead to great workplaces becoming the rule rather than the exception. And remembering that can keep the weariest of us going long past the point where we feel we should quit, literally and figuratively. Still, there are times when you may wonder if your leaders are truly in the way of your personal and managerial success. What to do then?

YOU AS AN EMPLOYEE, NOT A MANAGER

Except at the very top levels of an organization, most managers find they have a dual experience at work. The primary experience is appropriately that of manager, but during times of frustration and dejection—perhaps as a result of thwarted efforts to create a great workplace—their experience as an employee of the organization may take center stage. And employees who have exhausted all of their options, both in action and in belief, may determine

183

that leaving the organization is the only way to find validation for their contributions. By no means do we intend to provide advice for leaving your organization and finding a new path with more potential; there are other authors who are far better equipped to do so than we are. Rather, we want to normalize the experience of exasperation that arises when managers see the potential of their workplace, but are hamstrung in reaching it.

When studying great workplaces, indeed benchmarking your own against them, it is easy to believe that most people have work experiences characterized by trust, pride, and camaraderie. But to a great extent, that's not the case. In 2012, less than half of the employees surveyed by the Conference Board, a world-renowned research organization funded by its members, reported satisfaction with their jobs.[5] While we believe strongly that organizations will be forced, sooner rather than later, to address the environment in which their employees exist, there are many more companies on that journey than companies who have gotten close to anything resembling a destination. We simply haven't reached the critical mass to make the workplace imperative a foregone conclusion, just as we have with other voluntary efforts such as quality and customer service. While working toward a great workplace now undoubtedly will provide competitive advantages, market forces are not yet pushing your leaders to action.

And even if a better workplace is demanded by your stakeholders, your leaders may be well intentioned but not tuned in to the needs of employees. We worked with one company whose founders were absolutely convinced that the best thing they could do for employees was automatically enroll them in a 401(k) plan. They felt strongly that helping employees plan for retirement was the right thing to do. But the employees were largely single-income households with young children at home, and surveys and focus groups showed that what employees really wanted was more money in their paycheck. While their intention was good, the founders could have addressed it by offering retirement planning assistance or classes, which was more in line with the immediate priorities of their employees. All too often, the good intentions on the part of leaders just don't translate well in the absence of employee input.

Of course, some leaders, like those at Scripps Healthcare who launch periodic benefits surveys to ensure their decisions are hitting the mark, have turned the corner on participative management as an ordinary state of affairs. If your leaders have not, though, consider how their intentions may be driving the wrong action, and shift your own influence tactics appropriately.

We don't deny that there comes a point in every manager's career where they will consider the costs of staying to be higher than the costs of searching for another job—perhaps in a company that already has made great strides, but certainly in one that enables its managers to pursue a great workplace. But until that time comes, we encourage you to keep influencing your own workplace environment. That's what great workplace leaders do. Even if they don't have the circumstances that make the path forward particularly clear, they never stop trying.

WHAT TO DO NEXT

Whether you are attempting to influence your leaders to take action in the larger organization, or just working within your own work group or department, we have a number of suggested next steps, including:

○ Scout out managers in your organization who either have or are diligently working toward an environment of trust, pride, and camaraderie. Take them to lunch, or to coffee, and learn from their successes.

○ Create a community of practice with other interested managers in order to learn from one another, and possibly create momentum in the larger organization.

○ Find ways to communicate your success broadly, perhaps in company newsletters or discussion boards.

○ Visit www.mygreatworkplace.com and www.greatplacetowork.com for the most recent studies linking financial results to trust, pride, and camaraderie so you are fluent if the opportunity for influence arises.

○ Step into your own importance as the primary conduit of your employees' relationship to the organization. While your job description may not state it explicitly, anecdotal evidence abounds that your role is key to the employee experience.

○ Create an organizational identity scaled to your work group. Why does your department exist? What does it hope to do for the larger organization in service of value-creation for customers and society?

○ Get clear on your own priorities and make sure that creating a great workplace is one of them.

○ Spend more time focusing on what you can change than what you can't.

○ Share your opinions on organizational initiatives and operational changes, but also resolve to work with the team to meet them.

○ Examine the requirements of your role, and determine how to use them as opportunities to build trust, pride, and camaraderie.

CHAPTER 10

THE "ONE RULE" FOR EXCUSES

Through our experience writing this book, we've discovered a simple rule for dealing with the challenges to building a great workplace: "Don't resist. Channel the power of the challenge into your great workplace advantage."

In interview after interview with leaders at great workplaces, they reinforced our notion that attitude matters, and they discussed their own organization's identity as a cornerstone of their great workplace. We expected they'd be able to commiserate with the managers we encounter after workshops and in our consulting work who are weary and near-paralyzed by the size and scope of their obstacles. Surprisingly, great workplace leaders *didn't feel the weight of the challenges as much as we expected.* Rather, leaders see the challenges as stretch goals—intriguing in their enormity, but not impossible. This led us to understand the "great workplace judo" that leaders practice when it comes to their task—use the power and momentum of the challenge to your advantage.

We worked with a grocery chain several years ago. The chain operated with the excuse that the large proportion of younger and part-time workers, and consequent high turnover rate, was a challenge to their ever reaching "great" in the experience of their workplace. Yes, there are challenges here. It is harder to garner commitment when people see the job in your company as a waypoint to something else. High turnover compounds that problem by asking commitment of an ever-changing landscape of teammates.

But there are also advantages in those challenges. In our research, we find a clear "honeymoon effect" for employees who are on the job less than two years. The energy and eagerness that comes with starting a new job is an advantage many companies don't enjoy with such a large proportion of their population. Moreover, a part-time workforce allows for flexibility in scheduling that is unmatched in most companies. Actively harnessing these positive consequences may involve matching new, eager employees with more tenured employees to create formidable teams of energy and experience. Or emphasizing scheduling options in recruiting materials may help to recruit the best and brightest in a particular labor market segment.

Dig deeper to understand why the challenges exist, and you will see more clearly how to use them to your advantage. In this case, baggers and clerks worked part-time because they were high school and college students, and they often went on to careers in other fields entirely. The very particulars of this challenge help to inform ways to address it. An alumni association would be an ideal way to garner commitment, even among part-time and short-tenured staff. Not only could current employees see a clear path to one of many careers after their part-time job at the grocer, but alumni could continue their commitment and give back by serving as mentors and (if possible) customers.

In this case, treating the nature of employees solely as an obstacle means the manager resists and tries to reverse the situation by finding ways to recruit full-time and long-tenured employees. While admirable, it is unlikely that set of circumstances is going to change, and if it does, it certainly won't do so quickly.

Instead, the manager can save time and energy by doing two things: seeing and capitalizing on the opportunity in the challenge, and working with the flow of the challenge rather than against it.

THE OPPORTUNITY IN THE CHALLENGE

Several managers we spoke with found opportunities in challenges presented them, even when the challenges were quite consequential. The economic downturn meant many great workplaces had to consider layoffs (at worst) or a redeployment of their workforce (at best). But, though it was a wrenching period of time on the whole, great workplace managers told us that the key was to find the bright spot. One manager at Balfour Beatty Construction mused that optimism is not only productive, it sets you apart from competitors. "In this kind of economy, 75 percent of the folks are going to look for excuses, and 25 percent of the people are going to look for a reason to use the bad economy to make themselves better. I think we are definitely in that 25 percent. Instead of lamenting a bad economy, the conversations at Balfour Beatty are about how to better position ourselves for the future, and how to shift what we do to deliver the best value to this market."

Managers at NetApp agreed with that sentiment, adding that market changes, while rattling, also have a way of driving home key lessons about how to succeed where others have failed. "I think we had an opportunity to be inwardly focused in 2001–2002, with the economic downturn. Most of our customers in the Internet world were going away because of the dot-com bust. I think that was a catalyst for the executives and they were very aware that we could start to have multiple problems. It was their leadership that got us through that; they were completely focused on keeping the culture together." Sometimes the silver lining is a wake-up call to attend to the things that really matter to the organization's identity and ultimate success.

THE JUDO MOVE

Seeing the opportunity in the challenge is the first step, but truly great managers take it a step further, and use the challenge itself to their advantage. They move with the flow rather than swim against the current.

An organization's diversity, size, and global presence are all examples of turning challenge to one's advantage. At The Coca-Cola Company, their franchise model means there are a lot of managers who need to operate with standardized processes. Managing exceptions can be a challenge, unless you use those exceptions to make the whole operation better. A Coca-Cola manager told us, "Our bottlers actually make us better because they'll say no to something because it's actually not that good." Working hand-in-hand with your operation at the granular level can provide a rich pipeline of feedback for improvement, which wouldn't exist if that obstacle was resisted rather than channeled. Jill Smart, Chief Human Resources Officer at Accenture, also discussed how being a large, global organization can be used to a leader's advantage. "I think being big can work to your advantage. Big makes for more opportunities. For the generation coming in now, they want global experiences. That doesn't necessarily mean being an expatriate in another country anymore. Instead, they can do trainings with people from thirty different cultures and they learn about different cultures that way. Likewise, if I'm running an organization, I want to know where the best-run organizations are and I want to talk to the person about what they do and how they do it. The bigness, if you use it, it really is an advantage."

It is human nature to resist change, but the managers we interviewed were clear: Work with the challenge rather than against the challenge. Of course you can change the landscape over time, but great workplaces aren't about what can be done tomorrow. Rather, they *start* now. In his blog, marketing and leadership guru Seth Godin agrees: "We trust people because they showed up when it wasn't convenient, because they told the truth when it was easier to lie and because they kept a promise when they could have gotten away with breaking it. Every tough time and every pressured project is another opportunity to earn the trust of someone you care about."[1] Working with the challenge is easier said than done, to be sure. But before we leave you, we'll give you some specific suggestions about how to do just that.

WHAT TO DO NEXT

In the preceding chapters, we've presented concrete guidance about overcoming the challenges embedded in excuses, but we couldn't possibly have addressed every nuance of what you're facing. After adopting a productive attitude and clarifying your organization's identity, we'd recommend a three-step approach to addressing anything that's left over.

First, acknowledge the challenge. In every country, industry, organization, and work group, there are real obstacles to creating trust, pride, and camaraderie. Acknowledge that, and make peace with it. Go one step further and inventory all of the challenges you face in creating your great workplace, but only if you have the time, energy, and commitment to carry that inventory through the rest of the process. If not, you've simply created a list of excuses that will keep you stuck.

Second, clarify the challenge. Why does it exist? Is it a function of the reward systems in your work group, the organization's structure, or the unintended result of past decisions? You may use what is called the "five why" technique here, continuing to ask why until you are clear on the root of the problem. For example, you might proceed this way:

Challenge: It is difficult to generate commitment with my employees.

- *First why:* Many of them are part-time and temporary.
- *Second why:* Because they are students in high school or college and need flexibility.
- *Third why:* Because they have classes they need to take.
- *Fourth why:* Because they wish to graduate or get ahead.
- *Fifth why:* Because they are seeking to be successful.

Aha! So it's not that they're not committed. In fact, they want to be successful. How can we help them be successful?

In going through an exercise such as this, the opportunity in the challenge is uncovered—in this case, the caliber of employees that this manager has in his or her work group and their desire to be successful. Additionally, it provides the type of understanding that facilitates using it to your advantage—here, seeing how encouraging and supporting part-time work may create more loyalty from students, their family members, and the community at large.

Last but not least, reframe the challenge as an opportunity. If not immediately apparent after acknowledging and clarifying, the opportunity may be discovered through talking with other managers, ideally those in other industries or functional areas. Ask colleagues to complete this sentence: "I'd like to have your problems because . . ." Chances are, they are struggling with obstacles that seem intractable as well, but they may have the ability to see the silver lining in yours.

Another method, as Jill Smart from Accenture summarized, is to reverse the assumptions in the challenge. In her example, managers were having a hard time giving up locally held responsibilities that were to move to a centralized office (commonly called "shared services"). Managers rationalized why they should keep one operation or another, and conversation after conversation only turned up a small number of responsibilities that would move to a centralized office. Not enough responsibilities, in fact, to justify a centralized office. So, one of Jill's direct reports reversed the discussion. Instead of asking which operations would move, he suggested, "We're going to move *everything* to a shared service. Now you need to tell me what you need to keep locally." Reversing the conversation can produce movement where resistance often doesn't.

We've come to that "Wizard of Oz" moment in the book where what seemed difficult is actually very simple. We leave you with three thoughts.

- Adopt the rule of great workplaces: Treat every interaction as an opportunity to build trust, and that will overcome cognitive obstacles.
- Know yourself: Get clear on your work group and/or your organization's identity, and be sure you are acting in ways that reinforce that identity while allowing it to evolve to meet the needs of your environment.
- And, last but not least, acknowledge, clarify, and find the opportunity in the challenges you encounter, perhaps taking inspiration from the leaders and organizations featured in this book.

We wish you no excuses, and all the best on your journey to a great workplace.

NOTES

Introduction: Creating a Great Workplace

1. PricewaterhouseCoopers. "Global CEO Survey." http://www.pwc.com/gx/en/ceo-survey/index.jhtml. April, 2013.
2. Levering, R. L., and M. Moskowitz. *The 100 Best Companies to Work for in America.* Reading, MA: Addison Wesley, 1984.
3. Levering, Robert. *A Great Place to Work.* MTI Film & Video, 1990.

Chapter 1: The Anatomy of an Excuse

1. Faleye, Olubunmi, and Emery A. Trahan. "Labor-Friendly Corporate Practices: Is What Is Good for Employees Good for Shareholders?" *Journal of Business Ethics* 101, no. 1 (2011): 1–27.
2. Edmans, A. *Does the Stock Market Fully Value Intangibles? Employee Satisfaction and Equity Prices.* Philadelphia, PA: University of Pennsylvania, Wharton School, 2010.
3. Conley, Chip. "What We Measure Matters." http://www.huffingtonpost.com/chip-conley/what-we-measure-matters_b_204676.html. May, 2009.

Chapter 2: I Think [Like a Great Workplace Leader], Therefore I Am [a Great Workplace Leader]

1. Boyd, Robynne. "Do People Only Use 10 Percent of Their Brains?" http://www.scientificamerican.com/article.cfm?id=people-only-use-10-percent-of-brain. April, 2013.
2. Schein, Edgar H. "Organizational Culture." *American Psychologist* 45, no. 2 (February 1990): 109–119.

195

3. Rockwood, K. "Is Your Manager a Creativity Killer?" http://www
.fastcompany.com/1839167/your-manager-creativity-killer. June,
2012.

4. Rotter, J. B. (1966). "Generalized Expectancies for Internal Versus
External Control of Reinforcement." *Psychological Monographs: General and Applied*, 80, no. 1: 1–28.

5. Weiner, Bernard. "A Theory of Motivation for Some Classroom
Experiences." *Journal of Educational Psychology* 71, no. 1 (1979): 3.

6. Judge, Timothy A., Edwin A. Locke, Cathy C. Durham, and Avraham
N. Kluger. "Dispositional Effects on Job and Life Satisfaction: The
Role of Core Evaluations." *Journal of Applied Psychology* 83, no. 1
(1998): 17–34.

7. Collins, Jim. *Good to Great: Why Some Companies Make the Leap . . . and
Others Don't.* HarperBusiness, 2001.

8. Ariely, Dan. "The Fallacy of Supply and Demand." www.huffington-
post.com/dan-ariely/the-fallacy-of-supply-and_b_92590.html.
March, 2008.

9. Ainslie, George, and Nick Haslam. "Hyperbolic Discounting." *Choice
Over Time* (1992): 57–92.

10. HBR Blog Network. "Unilever's CEO on Making Responsible Business Work." http://blogs.hbr.org/ideacast/2012/05/unilevers-ceo
-on-making-respon.html.

11. Bruch, H., and S. Ghoshal. "Beware the Busy Manager." *Harvard
Business Review* 80, no. 2 (2002): 62.

Chapter 3: We Are What We Repeatedly Do

1. Peshwara, Rajeev. "Brains, Bones, and Nerves: The Only Three
Things an Enterprise Leader Should Focus On." http://changethis
.com/manifesto/show/84.03.BrainsBonesNerves. July, 2011.

2. Bernstein, Amy. "The Thought Leader Interview: Bill George."
http://www.strategy-business.com/article/07409?pg=all. November,
2007.

3. Kouzes, James M., and Barry Z. Posner. *The Leadership Challenge.* Vol.
3. Jossey-Bass, 2006.

4. Bruch, H., and S. Ghoshal. "Beware the Busy Manager." *Harvard Business Review* 80, no. 2 (2002): 62.

Chapter 4: I Didn't Have Enough Time to Do It Right

1. Leland, Karen. "New Study Shows We Are Overworked and Overwhelmed." http://www.huffingtonpost.com/karen-leland/employees-overworked_b_1553558.html. May, 2012.

2. Hewlett, Sylvia Ann, and Carolyn Buck Luce. "Extreme Jobs–The Dangerous Allure of the 70-Hour Workweek." *Harvard Business Review* 84, no. 12 (2006): 49–59.

3. Lally, Phillippa, Cornelia H. M. van Jaarsveld, Henry W. W. Potts, and Jane Wardle. "How Are Habits Formed: Modelling Habit Formation in the Real World." *European Journal of Social Psychology* 40, no. 6 (2010): 998–1009.

4. Duckworth, Angela L., Christopher Peterson, Michael D. Matthews, and Dennis R. Kelly. "Grit: Perseverance and Passion for Long-Term Goals." *Journal of Personality and Social Psychology* 92, no. 6 (2007): 1087.

5. Buckingham, Marcus. "The Frankenleader Fad." http://www.fastcompany.com/54132/frankenleader-fad. September, 2005.

6. Verplanken, Bas, and Wendy Wood. "Interventions to Break and Create Consumer Habits." *Journal of Public Policy & Marketing* (2006): 90–103.

7. Duhigg, Charles. *The Power of Habit: Why We Do What We Do in Life and Business.* Doubleday Canada, 2012.

8. Hodgson, Geoffrey. "The Nature and Replication of Routines." Unpublished manuscript http://www.gredeg.cnrs.fr/routines/workshop/papers/hodgson.pdf. 2004.

Chapter 5: That's Just Not My Job

1. IBM. "Global Chief Executive Officer Study: Leading Through Connections." http://www-935.ibm.com/services/us/en/c-suite/ceostudy2012/. April, 2012.

2. KPMG. "The 'War for Talent' Has Gone Digital—Is HR Ready?" http://www.kpmg.com/global/en/issuesandinsights/

articlespublications/press-releases/pages/human-resources-war-for-talent.aspx. October, 2012.

3. Pfeffer, Jeffrey. "Understanding Power in Organizations." *California Management Review* 34, no. 2 (1992): 29–50.

4. Bolman, Lee G., and Terrence E. Deal. *Reframing Organizations: Artistry, Choice and Leadership.* Wiley Desktop Editions, 2008.

5. Ibid.

Chapter 6: My Industry Is Different

1. Stoner, Charles R., Paul Stephens, and Matthew K. McGowan. "Connectivity and Work Dominance: Panacea or Pariah?" *Business Horizons* 52, no. 1 (2009): 67–78.

2. Arndt, Michael. "How O'Neill Got Alcoa Shining." http://www.businessweek.com/2001/01_06/b3718006.htm. February, 2001.

3. Barefoot, Kevin B., and Raymond J. Mataloni Jr. "U.S. Multinational Companies: Operations in the United States and Abroad in 2008." https://www.bea.gov/scb/pdf/2010/08%20August/0810_mncs.pdf. August, 2010.

Chapter 7: It's Just Not the Right Time

1. Harding, David, Satish Shankar, and Richard Jackson. "The Renaissance in Mergers and Acquisitions: The Surprising Lessons of the 2000s." http://www.bain.com/publications/articles/the-renaissance-in-mergers-and-acquisitions.aspx. January, 2013.

2. Christensen, Clayton M., and Richard Alton. "The New M&A Playbook." *Harvard Business Review* 89, no. 3 (2011): 48–57.

3. Sher, Robert. "Why Half of All M&A Deals Fail, and What You Can Do About It." http://www.forbes.com/sites/forbesleadershipforum/2012/03/19/why-half-of-all-ma-deals-fail-and-what-you-can-do-about-it/. March, 2012.

4. Cartwright, Susan, and Richard Schoenberg. "Thirty Years of Mergers and Acquisitions Research: Recent Advances and Future Opportunities." *British Journal of Management* 17, no. S1 (2006): S1–S5.

5. Favaro, Ken, Per-Ola Karlsson, and Gary Neilson. "CEO Succession Report: 12th Annual Global CEO Succession Study." http://www

.booz.com/media/uploads/BoozCo_CEO-Succession-Study-2011 _Extended-Study-Report.pdf.

6. Bureau of Labor Statistics. "Extended Mass Layoffs in 2011." http:// www.bls.gov/mls/mlsreport1039.pdf. December, 2012.

7. Makinen, Gail. *Economic Effects of 9/11: A Retrospective Assessment.* DIANE Publishing, 2011.

8. Knowledge@Wharton. "North American Businesses Hurt Most by Arab Spring." http://www.bls.gov/mls/mlsreport1039.pdf. January, 2012.

9. Selye, Hans. "The General Adaptation Syndrome and the Diseases of Adaptation." *The Journal of Clinical Endocrinology* 6, no. 2 (1946): 117–230.

10. Weiss, Howard M., and Russell Cropanzano. "Affective Events Theory: A Theoretical Discussion of the Structure, Causes and Consequences of Affective Experiences at Work." In Staw, Barry M., and L. L. Cummings (Eds.). *Research in Organizational Behavior: An Annual Series of Analytical Essays and Critical Reviews, Vol. 18.* (pp. 1–74). Science/JAI Press, 1996.

11. Kusstatscher, Verena, and Cary L. Cooper. *Managing Emotions in Mergers and Acquisitions.* Edward Elgar Pub, 2005.

Chapter 8: I'd Be a Great People Manager if It Weren't for All the People

1. OECD. "Trade Union Density." http://stats.oecd.org/Index.aspx? DataSetCode=UN_DEN. April, 2013.

2. Jones, Jeffrey. "In U.S., Labor Union Approval Steady at 52%." http://www.gallup.com/poll/157025/labor-union-approval-steady .aspx. August, 2012.

3. Bureau of Labor Statistics. "Union Membership Declines in 2012." http://www.bls.gov/opub/ted/2013/ted_20130124.htm. January, 2013.

Chapter 9: My Boss Ate My Homework

1. Human Capital Institute. "HR Trends & Priorities for 2013." http:// www.hci.org/files/field_slides/HCI_McLeanCo_TrendsPriorities 2013_11513.pdf. January, 2013.

2. HBR Blog Network. "Positive Deviance and Unlikely Innovators." http://blogs.hbr.org/ideacast/2010/06/positive-deviance-and-unlikely.html. June, 2010.

3. Mackey, John, Raj Sisodia, and Bill George. *Conscious Capitalism: Liberating the Heroic Spirit of Business.* Harvard Business School Press, 2013.

4. Covey, Stephen. *The Seven Habits of Highly Successful People.* Simon & Schuster, 1989.

5. Ray, Rebecca, and Thomas Rizzacasa. "Job Satisfaction: 2012 Edition." http://www.conference-board.org/publications/publicationdetail.cfm?publicationid=2258&topicid=40&subtopicid=160. June, 2012.

Chapter 10: The "One Rule" for Excuses

1. http://randomolio.com/2013/04/10/why-should-i-trust-you/

ACKNOWLEDGMENTS

First and foremost, we are indebted to the people at each organization that generously shared with us their time, their stories, and their insights. We interviewed leaders and employees at Accenture, Alston & Bird, Balfour Beatty, The Coca-Cola Company, Devon Energy, Mayo Clinic, NetApp, Teach for America, Whole Foods Market, and Zappos. We left each interview inspired by the leaders with whom we spoke. Their unwavering dedication to great workplaces and the actions they took to create and maintain trust, pride, and camaraderie was a wellspring of rich examples and recommendations included throughout this book.

Countless people supported us in this second writing endeavor, at Jossey-Bass and at Great Place to Work® Institute. We thank them all, specifically Genoveva Llosa and John Maas for being our cheerleaders, our taskmasters, and our touch points in getting this book's message out into the world. We are also grateful to have continued to learn from Jenna Land Free at Girl Friday Productions while writing this book. Though separated by a few thousand miles, comments in the margins and periodic phone calls made it seem like she was at the table (conference or kitchen) as we worked. Jenna, our book is once again better due to your involvement.

At Great Place to Work® Institute, we thank its cofounders Robert Levering and Amy Lyman, for continuing to support our efforts to spread the message that any company can be a great place to work. Thank you to our esteemed colleagues at the Institute—in San Francisco, New York, and around the world—many of whom read drafts, answered questions, provided insights, and otherwise kept us going even when the going got tough. A big shout-out goes to Lexi Gibson, project manager extraordinaire and all around delightful human being, for her dedication to this project.

From Jennifer: I'd also like to thank my colleagues in the Foster College of Business and my friends all over the country for their support in writing this book. I am grateful to faculty in my department, for encouraging my continued success in translating research and experience for a managerial audience. Special thanks to Larry Weinzimmer and Valerie Pape. Your inhuman patience while collaborating with an author under deadline was nothing short of remarkable. Gratitude also goes to my personal board of directors, people who have no shortage of both supportive words and tough love—Stacy, Erin, Suzanne, Stephenie, Angela, Stacey, Becky, and Yvonne. You always asked, "How are you?," even when you knew it was a loaded question. Last but not least, thank you to my family in Davenport, who continue to support my success even as they remind me I'd be loved regardless. Special thanks to my nieces Matilda and Wenonah, who I'm convinced will grow up and change the world in ways I can't even imagine. Go girls!

From Michael: I'd like to thank my colleagues and friends for their guidance, support and patience. José Tolovi, Jr., Susan Lucas Conwell, and Robert Levering gave me the space and encouragement to focus on this project, and my colleagues on the corporate and U.S. teams have been exceedingly patient with me as I juggled multiple responsibilities. Special thanks to David Robert, friend and business partner, who continues to model for me the type of leader I wish to become. Much appreciation to my mentors who have guided me along in this endeavor: Carol, Linda, Pat, Dawn, Donna, Brooke, and Jennifer. And thank you to my dad, James Burchell, who is always there with his unconditional love and support.

ABOUT THE AUTHORS

Jennifer Robin, Ph.D., is a Research Fellow at Great Place to Work® Institute. A former consultant with the Institute, she led the Advisory Practice, helping senior leaders integrate their organization's culture with its strategy and aligning efforts to be a great workplace. Currently, Jennifer teaches in undergraduate, MBA, and professional programs in the Foster College of Business at Bradley University. She serves as an adjunct consultant for the Institute and conducts research on the importance of values and stories to organizational culture and the leader behaviors that build trust.

Jennifer holds a Ph.D. in Industrial/Organizational Psychology from the University of Tennessee and undergraduate degrees in both Human Resource Management and Psychology from the University of Northern Iowa. In her spare time, Jennifer can be found on hiking trails, in airports, or spoiling her nieces.

Michael Burchell, Ed.D., is Vice President, International Operations at Great Place to Work® Institute. A member of the corporate management team, Michael oversees affiliate operations, global expansion efforts, and the business development of multinational clients across the Great Place to Work® network.

Previously, Michael led consulting services for the Institute in the United States. He also co-owns and is a director for Great Place to Work® Institute in the United Arab Emirates based in Dubai.

Prior to joining the Institute, Michael worked at W. L. Gore & Associates, and the University of Massachusetts. Michael received his doctorate from the University of Massachusetts Amherst, and also holds degrees from Colorado State University and the University of Southern California. Michael's address is in Washington, DC, but he lives in seat 8A on flights to various destinations around the globe.

Great Place to Work® Institute is a global research, consulting, and training firm that helps organizations identify, create, and sustain great workplaces through the development of high-trust workplace cultures. The Institute serves businesses, non-profits and government agencies from forty-one affiliate offices covering more than forty-five countries.

Co-founded by bestselling business author Robert Levering and organizational consultant Amy Lyman, Ph.D., in collaboration with a team of professionals committed to the recognition and development of great workplaces around the world, the Institute's mission is to build a better society by helping companies transform their workplaces. Great Place to Work® clients are those companies and organizations that wish to maintain Best Company environments, those that are ready to dramatically improve the culture within their workplaces, and those in between the two. The Institute believes that organizations that build trust and create a rewarding cycle of personal contribution and appreciation create workplace cultures that deliver outstanding business performance.